Praise for

Whitecentricism and Linguoracism Exposed

"Using his own experiences growing up poor in Haiti as a jumping off point, Pierre W. Orelus strikes at the heart of racism and colonization through sharp political, cultural, educational, and historical analysis. Simply put, *Whitecentricism and Linguoracism Exposed* is a powerful book that anyone seriously interested in understanding systemic racial inequality in the United States and its de-facto colonies will want to read."
—Wayne Au, Assistant Professor of Education at the University of Washington-Bothell, author of *Critical Curriculum Studies: Education, Consciousness, and the Politics of Knowing*, and an editor for *Rethinking Schools*

"Pierre W. Orelus's present work creates a critical space of counter-racism awareness that should minimally confront Whitecentricism and its still-colonizing life prospects at historical, descriptive, and analytical levels… It should be widely read, for it guides us to a more humanist space that embraces the rights of all for the benefit of all."
From the foreword, Ali Abdi, Professor of Education and International Development at the University of Alberta in Edmonton, Canada

"In this engaging, accessible, and thoughtful book, Pierre W. Orelus reveals the price we all pay for the enduring pathologies of whitecentricism and linguoracism. These practices that relegate people of different races to radically different life chances can be remedied, Orelus argues, but only by sincere and serious efforts to change the ways we teach, learn, think, and speak. As much a guide to a new and better world as an analysis of the shortcomings of the one we now inhabit, this is a book that can teach us how to do serious work and do it well."
—George Lipsitz, author of *How Racism Takes Place*

Whitecentricism and Linguoracism Exposed

Darren E. Lund, Paul R. Carr, and Virginia Lea
Series Editors

Vol. 4

The Critical Multicultural Perspectives on Whiteness series
is part of the Peter Lang Education list.
Every volume is peer reviewed and meets
the highest quality standards for content and production.

PETER LANG
New York • Washington, D.C./Baltimore • Bern
Frankfurt • Berlin • Brussels • Vienna • Oxford

PIERRE W. ORELUS

Whitecentricism and Linguoracism Exposed

Towards the De-centering of Whiteness and Decolonization of Schools

PETER LANG
New York • Washington, D.C./Baltimore • Bern
Frankfurt • Berlin • Brussels • Vienna • Oxford

Library of Congress Cataloging-in-Publication Data
Orelus, Pierre W.
Whitecentricism and linguoracism exposed: towards the de-centering of whiteness and
decolonization of schools / Pierre W. Orelus.
pages cm. — (Critical multicultural perspectives on whiteness; vol. 4)
Includes bibliographical references and index.
1. Racism. 2. Racism in education.
3. Racism in language. 4. Decolonization. I. Title.
HT1521.O825   305.8—dc23   2013003885
ISBN 978-1-4331-1983-5 (hardcover)
ISBN 978-1-4331-1982-8 (paperback)
ISBN 978-1-4539-1115-0 (e-book)
ISSN 2166-8507

Bibliographic information published by **Die Deutsche Nationalbibliothek**.
Die Deutsche Nationalbibliothek lists this publication in the "Deutsche
Nationalbibliografie"; detailed bibliographic data is available
on the Internet at http://dnb.d-nb.de/.

The paper in this book meets the guidelines for permanence and durability
of the Committee on Production Guidelines for Book Longevity
of the Council of Library Resources.

© 2013 Peter Lang Publishing, Inc., New York
29 Broadway, 18th floor, New York, NY 10006
www.peterlang.com

All rights reserved.
Reprint or reproduction, even partially, in all forms such as microfilm,
xerography, microfiche, microcard, and offset strictly prohibited.

Printed in the United States of America

Table of Contents

Acknowledgments   vii
Foreword
Ali A. Abdi   ix
Introduction: xiii
Chapter 1
   Whitecentricism Exposed: De-centering Whiteness for a More
   Racially Inclusive Society   1
Chapter 2
   Being Black and Brown in a White World: Challenges and
   Possibilities   13
Chapter 3
   Reframing the Debate on Democratic, Educational,
   and Linguistic Rights of Minorities   29
Chapter 4
   Decolonizing Schools and Our Mentality: Counter
   Narratives from a Colonized Subject   41
Chapter 5
   Beyond Linguoracism and White Hegemony:
   Affirming Multiple Identities and Languages   53

Conclusion	67
Epilogue:	
The Unfinished Business of Decolonization: A Dialogue with Pierre Wilbert Orelus	71
Bibliography	85
Index	95

Acknowledgments

This book would not have been a reality without the support of many people. First, I want to thank Paul Carr, Virginia Lee, and Darren Lund for giving me the opportunity to publish this book in their series. Paul, Virginia, and Darren provided constructive feedback on the first draft of the manuscript. In addition, they edited many parts of it. Thank you colleagues! You rock!

Second, I am deeply indebted to Professor Ali Abdi for writing the foreword and Professors George Lipsitz and Wayne Au for writing a blurb endorsing this book. Third, I am forever grateful to my wife and the mother of our beloved daughter, Romina Pacheco. Romina has been instrumental in most of my academic and professional accomplishments. You rock sista!

Fourth, I want to thank my mother, Leanne Adelson, who never forgets to pray for and inspires me everyday to become much more resilient and much stronger, and my daughter, Asha, who makes me smile and happy everyday with her curiosity and great imagination. Fifth, I wish to thank my brother, Lyonel Orelus, and my sister, Frida Orelus, who have supported me throughout the years. They are exceptional siblings. Sixth, I want to thank the staff at Peter Lang for their hard work, particularly Chris Meyer and Bernadette Shade, and Saba Wear for designing the cover of the book. Saba is a brilliant artist.

Seventh, I want to thank my students and some of my colleagues at New Mexico State University who have taught me many things about linguicism and whitecentricism. Through dialogue in class and other settings, I have learned a lot from them about these two forms of oppression. Finally, I am grateful to the almighty who has given me the strength to write about and stand up against various forms of oppression, namely institutional racism, whitecentricism, linguoracism, xenophobia, and micro-aggression.

Foreword

ALI A. ABDI

In this important and timely book, Pierre Orelus deals with an issue that is immediate and interactively located within the lived contexts of the majority of the world's population. Although racism on the basis of skin color was not recorded before the fateful voyages of Christopher Columbus and other wealth and power-hungry Europeans hordes who descended on the lands of other people, the issue of white supremacy, or Whitecentricism as the author rightly calls it, has been in full force since then. As Gary Taylor (2004), in his important work, *Buying Whiteness: Race, Culture and Identity from Columbus to Hip-hop*, noted, high and low categorizations of humanity have been the practice of European racism for the past 520 years. So racism, especially against black people, has achieved a remarkable temporal endurance, mainly because it is not only a project of mass oppression, but, by being so, it extensively privileges the lives of those who practice it.

Technically, therefore, Whitecentricism, linguoracism, and their affiliated categories are very complex projects that must be deconstructed to viably reconstruct the onto-existential de-humanizations of peoples of African descent in Africa, as well as in the diaspora. As Orelus rightly notes, to counter the problems, we need to aim for and achieve full projects of decolonization and inclusive democratic lives that can show possibilities of other possible contexts. Basically, until the basis of the case (i.e., Whitecentricism) is effectively dealt with, the desired deconstructions of the categories will not happen. In this short foreword, therefore, and as a way of aiming for some concise impact but also as a way of commenting on the book's topical center, I intentionally stay more with an analysis of the realities of Whitecentricism. Indeed, the projects of slavery and colonization were purely theorized and practiced on the basis of this false superiority in which those who at one point in world history had some control over the lives of others systematically demeaned and mentally destroyed the being of those others.

It is via this reality that Whitecentricism successfully proved one thing: its practitioners are extensively disposed to oppress and, when convenient, annihilate the existentialities of their fellow humans. Interestingly and to be observationally fair, the inter-white project of slavery and all around de-humanizations have also been so extensive that, when one counts it right, there may be more white slaves, enslaved of course, by other whites, than black slaves in human history. Yet, the mental and corporeal destructive forces of slavery seem more effectively attached to Africans, mainly because, I would suggest, history is now practiced by many, including non-black non-whites, via the cruel lenses of anti-black racism and its sponsorship via Whitecentricism.

With this life fact, the massive and mad global jailhouse racism built encircles us and continually lessens the space of breathability that those who of us who are yearning for some salvation from its cruel stranglehold are seeking. Pierre Orelus's present work creates a critical space of counter-racism awareness that should minimally confront Whitecentricism and its still-colonizing life prospects at historical, descriptive, and analytical levels. Indeed, the dominant intersections of racism and the way it negatively or positively intersects with the lives of people (depending on one's thickness of skin pigmentation) is so dominant in even so-called Western democracies that doing the work to dissect its constructions, structure, and outcomes should be the *sine qua non* for the probable survivability of those who are, so widely and without shelter, exposed to it.

The issue of survivability is indeed important in that Orelus himself rightly relays the temporal urgency of doing this scholarly deed before he could be overwhelmed one way or another by, among other ailments or purely by itself, the hitherto incurable pathology of racism. In reading those points, I was reminded of other African, anti-racist campaigners and freedom fighters (in physical or intellectual/artistic terms) who, *ipso facto*, showed such urgency: the likes of Frantz Fanon, Steve Biko, Bob Marley, and Okot p'Biket, all disengaged from life while young, but the anti-racist, anti-colonial, anti-dehumanization, anti-anti-persona Africana legacies they left behind have formed a very thick body of libratory praxes that has affirmed, for especially African youth (whether in the continent, in Haiti, in Jamaica, in North America, in highly skin color conscious Latin America, or in the poor boroughs of Africa-built London) who have been lied to with respect to their histories, cultures, and their overall worth and fundamental, indeed natural rights to claim a stake on intelligence, achievement, and beauty, as well as the central self-esteem/self-efficacy life conjecture that Bob Marley so powerfully sang about and Aimé Césaire (1972) so poignantly, but determinedly, wrote about.

By multi-directionally and multi-perspectively engaging in this quasi-autobiographical scholarly work, Pierre Orelus has clearly seen so much of "IT": racism and its affiliated practices are, today, as systematically constructed and applied as ever, and they are state-wise and institutionally entrenched. Some say these happen in subtle ways now, but those of us who confront it on daily basis on the common street and surely in many private locales or occasionally via the snobbish gentility of few refined Whitecentrics (and yes, in the ontologies of the colonized who, in the very active ways the colonizer taught them, complemented by their suppressed consciences, counter-reflectively discriminate against their fellow Africans who remind them of their own lowered historic-cultural location, their ascribed failure and shame (Frantz Fanon's magisterial work, *Black Skin, White Masks* (1967), will be very helpful here)) expansively understand what it looks like and how it is deployed for maximum impact.

Yes, the author's descriptions of Haiti and the elevating of the usually sullen lives of theoretically "God-fearing" missionaries, by the poor Haitians themselves, are symptomatic of these frightening internalizations of heavy doses of ontological inferioritizations still wreaking havoc on the beings of the global sub-subaltern. As complicated as that fact is, the *longue durée* project of demeaned and self-demeaning subjectivities was/is not limited to the inter-black/white contexts, but Whitecentricism has also spawned a cluster of other skin pigmentation considerations that have forced some to seek solace in the extent in which they are removed from blackness, which can pragmatically explain the author's experiences in Venezuela, where the young girl's affirmation "*a mi no me gusta a los negros*" is a tiny component of the well-known story in Latin America in which an important mission in life could be becoming as "white" as possible and as non-negro as possible.

In Canada, where I live, this may be reflected in few informal conversations I had with some African Canadian academics in which we casually discussed (although nothing is casual about the situation) how some minorities in the country complain about what they vociferously call "white racism," when they themselves launch so much racism against darker cultural communities. All of this, when in actuality, the "R" word and its painful practices have no biological foundations that could justify them. Indeed, as Michael Cook in his seminal work, *A Brief*

History of the Human Race (2005), has so cogently noted, with the inter-human species-based difference so minute, racism scientifically becomes a form of auto-racism in which the racist, to the analytical delight of some of us, is actually practicing the act against herself/himself.

All of that, however, is not enough deterrent for those who know they will benefit from Whitecentricism and its lately forming adjunct statuses. Indeed, the wide cartographies of the story do not seem to be contracting that much, and Pierre Orelus' intervening and critical work thickly interrogates the problematic constructions, practices, and outcomes of the case and calls for a more inclusive and humanist perspective that liberates us all from the nightmare of racism and falsely established categorizations of the *persona humana*. In sum, this is a fine book that should benefit students and scholars of history, education, culture, and the critical study of human relations and inter-human aspirations. It should be widely read, for it guides us to a more humanist space that embraces the rights of all for the benefit of all.

Introduction

Do Not Mistake My Confidence for Arrogance

No sir, no madam, it is not insolence or arrogance
Nor is it anger; it is nothing but full confidence
You did not expect me to be assertive and confident
So you label me as being too cocky and overconfident
I do not allow factors such as race and gender dictate how I behave and talk
It is too bad you base on these factors to judge the way I speak or walk
It is not really my problem if you read me through whitecentric views or lenses
I will still be assertive, and your prejudice will not cause me lose my senses
I know, I know during slavery and colonization
My ancestors were not allowed to any form of assertion
They were only expected to shut up and allow themselves to be oppressed
They were not allowed to say anything that would make the masters feel stressed
My ancestors were expected to be hard workers, extremely polite, and submissive

Their children were also expected to be obedient, to work hard, and to be passive
My ancestors were warriors who fought against their oppressors and won
Despite their courage, resilience, and brilliance, they were still badly put down
As their offspring, I am not expected to show a strong sense of self-empowerment
Nor am I expected to challenge those in power unless I do not mind ill treatment
When I talk with confidence, I am often seen and read as being arrogant
As the descendant of slaves and colonized, I am not expected to be elegant
A strong sense of self-affirmation is not expected of the marginalized
This is a historical factor that needs be critically explored and analyzed
As for men and women of color, many labels have been placed on their identity
And this has been done repeatedly to them for centuries. This is just insanity
Yes, I am black, brown, and proud, and I am not afraid of asserting my self
I do not suffer of insecurity, and paranoia certainly does not absolve my inner self
Do not mistake my confidence for arrogance and my passion for aggressiveness
My way of talking and my words deeply reflect my strong sense of self-assertiveness

Those who know define racism as discrimination by a group against another for the purposes of subjugation or maintaining subjugation. In other words, one cannot be a racist unless one has the power to subjugate. What blacks are doing is merely to respond to a situation in which they find themselves the objects of white racism. We are in the position in which we are because of our skin. We are collectively segregated against—what can be more logical than for us to respond as a group? (Biko, 2007, p. 27)

All forms of social inequality are defined by class relations or motivated by the persistent drive to perpetuate class inequality within the context of the capitalist state, a phenomenon perpetuated by the ongoing construction and reconstruction of capitalist class relations. Thus, racism is operationalized through racialized class relations. Sexism is operationalized through gendered class relations. Heterosexism is operationalized through homophobic class relations. All these function in concert to sustain cultural, political, and economic stratification within societies at large. (Darder, 2011, p. 119)

White Supremacy is the unnamed political system that has made the modern world what is today. (Mills, 1997, p.1)

This book is part of a larger social justice project aimed at raising consciousness about the racial, educational, and socioeconomic conditions of black and brown people, including linguistically and racially diverse students, in a white world. Specifically, this book unveils and challenges the hegemony of whiteness and intersecting forms of oppression, such as linguistic, class, racial, and gender oppression, that have limited the life chances of people of color. By adopting this intersectional approach, this book challenges binaries and dichotomies preventing people from seeing the connected manner in which race, class, language, and gender factors affect people of color (Crenshaw, 1993; Rothenberg, 2007).

At the outset, it is important to make the following statements: This book spans almost a decade of my writing, teaching, and learning experiences as a man of color. Some parts critically and deeply reflect my ontological and professional journey, and such a journey is situated in a larger socio-political, racial, and cultural context of the Americas. As such, I begin by providing a short autoethnographical account of my lived experience, for I believe the personal is also political (Holman Jones, 2005).

Witnessing and Experiencing Race, Class, and Gender Stratification

As I have asserted in my previous work (Orelus, 2007, 2010) and in numerous talks I have given at universities across the United States, Latin America, and Europe, I did not know what it was like to be a black man until I moved to the United States about 2 decades ago. In my native land, Haiti, colorism matters a great deal and impacts the livelihood of those who have dark skin and are poor. As I argue elsewhere (Orelus, forthcoming), "Generally in Haiti, those who are light-skinned tend to be appreciated and receive more attention than those who are dark-skinned." However, while living there, I was primarily concerned with class and gender inequalities, not racial discrimination.

Given my poor working-class background, I did not need lectures on, courses on Marxism, or to conduct research on social-class issues to fully understand what it is like to experience abject poverty. Poverty was so rampant in my social milieu that I breathed it almost every day and everywhere, at the underfunded schools I attended, in the schoolyard where I played soccer with my poor working-class classmates and friends, and in the poor neighborhood in which I hung out with my friends and siblings. At a young age, 6 or younger, I already knew the difference between those who were poor and those who were not.

By visiting close friends and classmates living in marginalized places, such as Cité Soleil, known as the most impoverished and "dangerous" city in Haiti, and comparing these places to the "good," "clean," and "safe" neighborhoods in which the rich lived, I was able to have a clear sense of class disparity. Moreover, by attending a poorly funded public high school located next to a well-resourced private high school, it was not hard to distinguish the poor Haitian students from those who were privileged. The rich students wore nice clothes and shoes and were often dropped off and picked up by parents driving fancy cars, whereas the poor students often wore threadbare clothes and walked miles to and from their schools. I was one of the poor students, as were many of my close friends. I often had to go to school hungry. This experience helped me understand what it is like to be subjected to an extreme form of poverty.

Finally, witnessing my poor single mother raising four of us in a tiny, dilapidated house located in the poor and underdeveloped rural area of Beauge with no access to electricity and clean water and almost no support from my father helped me develop critical awareness and consciousness about class issues and the harmful effect of sexism on women, particularly poor women. I knew many women in my neighborhood who worked hard to feed their families, including their husbands, yet were often beaten by those husbands for no apparent reason; this created a sense of urgency in me to write about male arrogance and domination, which I have discussed in previous books (Orelus, 2009, 2011b).

Why Write This Book at This Present Time?

Before deciding to embark on the journey of writing this book, I asked myself many questions: Why write this book at this present time? Why not later? After critically examining the thoughts and feelings that prompted these questions, I asked myself further questions: Why not? What if I die young like many black people? If I want to be true to myself, I must admit that the fear or feeling that I might die young sometimes crosses my mind, although I do not have a logical explanation for this fear or feeling.

The best possible way I can interpret such a fear is that many young black men have died as a result of a massive heart attack (see the documentary *The Angry Heart: The Impact of Racism on Heart Disease Among African Americans*, 2010). Their deaths have forced me to think seriously about my own life as a black man, for I know that institutional racism—manifested in the forms of racial profiling, micro-aggression (Solorzano, 1998), denial of employment and job promotion opportunities, and lack of access to quality education and health care—has caused people of color to develop high blood pressure, diabetes, and heart disease, among other health problems, leading to their savage, early deaths (Kozol, 1985, 1991).

As an example, I knew a healthy-looking and health-conscious black lawyer and community organizer who died of a massive heart attack about 3 years ago, when he was only 41 years old. Close friends and relatives were shocked by his sudden death, for no one in his family had died of a heart attack. Some have speculated that the massive heart attack that took his life may have been stemmed from racial fatigue caused by institutional racism he experienced as a lawyer and community activist.

Such a speculation makes sense to me as a black man who has been experiencing both racial fatigue and micro aggression too frequently. As Dei, Karumanchery, and Karumanchery-Luik (2004) have pointed out, these forms of oppression have affected the health of many black people, young and old, and I am not an exception. The root causes of heart attack that have taken the lives of many people of color might be hard for some to understand, especially those who do not have much awareness about the profound way in which institutional racism has made people of color sick. For example, those with white privileges who lack awareness might not know the ways and the degree to which institutional racism has impacted the life of people of color (Dei, 1996, 1999, 2009a). However, for people of color, this is not hard to comprehend, for they have been victims of this form of racism in their daily lives.

Admittedly, fearing I might die young from racial fatigue rooted in institutional racism has led me to write this book now rather than wait. Research shows the life expectancy of black people living in the United States is less than their white counterparts (Bonilla-Silva, 2003, 2010), although, depending on social class, some black people might live longer than others. Racism is epidemic and has unquestionably affected the lives of people of African descent in many ways—psychologically, emotionally, educationally, socio-economically, and politically.

In the following section, I use the word *burden* as a metaphor to articulate many forms of oppression to which people of color have been subjected in the United States. My use of the word *burden* may appear controversial. However, I must say that I could not think of a more fitting word to talk pointedly about the experience of people of color with Whitecentricism, which will be defined later, institutional racism, and classism. I explain in detail what I mean, for example, by "the burden of being a Person of Color." I draw on family rituals and ontological experience to contextually situate and explicate the underlying reasons that led me to use the word *burden*. I examine the way and the extent to which the word *burden* reflects and applies, for example, to the daily reality of black and brown people.

The Burden of Being a Person of Color in a Self-proclaimed Democratic Country

How can being a Person of Color feel like a burden in the most self-proclaimed democratic country in the Western world (Carr, 2011; West, 2004), the United States? Before attempting to explore and answer this question, let me first acknowledge that I am fully cognizant of the fact that the word *burden* has negative connotations. This word has never been used to refer to anything positive. Rather, it has been utilized to refer to things that are annoying or unbearable that a person does not want to deal with. For example, it is a burden having to do something that a person does not want to do, such as working at assembly-line factories, sweatshops, or in sugarcane and cotton plantations during slavery. It is also a burden having to move from one place to another or to sleep from one house to another to save a person's life from civil wars or genocide.

Thus, associating the word *burden* with people of color, particularly black people, makes matters worse, given that historically negative phrases or words, such as *black market*, *blackmail*, *blacklist*, and *blackout*, among others, have been associated with the word blackness or black. Therefore, one might rightfully ask: Why does the author use the word *burden* in this Introduction? Is this word not negatively connected with blackness? Is this not disrespectful to the pioneers of the negritude and the civil rights movements and the Black Panthers who have inspired billions of blacks around the world to strive to heighten the value and the beauty of the black race while battling racism, imperialism, and colonialism? Is not doing so perpetuating in some way the negative stereotypes and images about black people that have been historically circulated in the media, schools, and society in general? In short, is using the word *burden* in this context not offensive to all black people? To those rightfully asking these questions, I feel that, as the author, I owe them an explanation regarding my use of the word *burden*. To this end, I wish to begin with a story embedded in a family ritual that has shaped my childhood, adolescence, and adulthood.

I am reminded that, when I was a boy, my mother quite often used the French word *fardeau*, meaning burden, while praying and talking aloud about her economic, social, and emotional tribulations as a single mother raising four children. She often cried while reading her bible, singing, and praying at night. She would say, "Oh God! Please help me lift this or that burden. I am no longer able to carry it. I am tired. I am exhausted. Please God, help me carry this burden." She would also call on her deceased mother whose spirit she trusted to protect her and give her the desperately needed strength to continue her long journey as a single mother. She would pray every night before she went to bed and at dawn before she started her long day as a street vendor.

As a boy who was still naïve and could not make sense of the content of my mother's nightly and daily ritual, I often asked her why she was crying. She would respond, "I am okay, my son," and she would then continue to cry while praying and using the word *burden*. She never took the time to explain why she burst into tears while praying. Perhaps, she assumed that I was too young and I would not understand what she was going through. Or perhaps she did not want to make me sad. My mother always tried to make her children happy by trying hard to provide for them, despite her miserable economic condition. At times, I would cry when I saw her crying. She would then stop crying and try to console me, but she never explained why she used the word *burden* while praying and crying. This was a family ritual that is deeply registered in my mind. In many ways, this is the story I was born into and grew up with.

It has been more than 20 years since I have had a chance to witness and be a part of this family ritual I grew up with. Because I have been facing countless racial challenges as a US naturalized black citizen, I have learned to appreciate this ritual at a deeper level. I was particularly fascinated and touched by its spiritual depth and revelation of the socio-economic and emotional problems my single mother was facing at the time. This ritual has become part of my spiritual life in the sense that, each time I am confronted with racial, family, and socio-economic challenges, I say a prayer, silently asking visible and invisible spiritual forces to help me remain strong and show me ways to solve these challenges.

Although my mother used the word *burden* to refer to her daily socioeconomic and emotional challenges as a single parent of four children, I use it here only to refer to the daily ill treatment, racial aggression, and other forms of racially motivated oppression that people of color have faced in their daily lives. At the same time, it is important to point out that, by using this word, my intention is not to generalize the daily reality of black people, as there are many differences among black people due to their immigrant status, gender, social class, sexuality, status, language, (dis)ability, and age, among others. For example, the daily burden of an African American might not be the same as a poor black immigrant. Likewise, the lived experience of an able-bodied black person is not the same as that of a physically, emotionally, and psychologically challenged black person. Further, the daily challenges of a poor and/or gay, bisexual, transgender black person is not same as a heterosexual and middle- or upper-class black person. Finally, being an able-bodied, young, heterosexual black professor, writer, and researcher is not the same as being an old, black, gay professor, writer, or researcher because of the homophobic and ageist world in which we live. Although the former might be primarily concerned with racism, the latter also has to deal with racism, ageism, and homophobia.

These factors matter across racial lines. For example, just as black people may experience classism, sexism, ageism, and heterosexism, so do white people. No racial group is exempt from these forms of oppression, thus, explaining the common human thread and struggle that binds us as humans, despite the social construction of our race. As far as my personal social class trajectory is concerned, I say that my experience working as a dishwasher in nursing homes and hotels and as a housekeeper at malls when I first arrived in the United States is not the same as being a university professor, a writer, and a researcher. However, like many professors of color, my class privileges have not and will not protect me from individual and institutional racism and white supremacy. In other words, my social class status can change, and it has changed. However, I can never change the fact that I am black and that some people will discriminate against me because of my blackness. This realization has led me to conclude that the weight of race and racism that professors of color and other black and brown professionals have been forced to carry on their shoulders throughout their journey in the white world might be heavier than that of class and classism.

Having provided this rationale regarding my use of the word *burden*, I now return to the question: How does being a person of color feel like a burden in the most self-proclaimed democratic country in the Western world, the United States? The answer(s) to this question varies depending on a person's existential and personal experiences. Before proceeding with my analysis, let me make it clear that it is not a person's blackness or brownness that is the burden. Rather, it is the daily struggle dealing with oppressive forms of racism and white supremacy that feel like a burden to many black and brown people living in a white world. For example, it is a burden having to constantly worry about racial profiling, such as being pulled over by police officers who choose to pull a person over merely because they assume that person might have drugs or guns in the car or being followed in stores to see if a non-white person is shoplifting.

Also, is it not also a burden to worry about being falsely convicted and unfairly thrown in jail, running the risk of receiving the death penalty, for a crime a person did not commit? As I write this book, the controversial case of an African

American man, Troy Davis, made the headlines. According to popular opinion, Davis was unfairly executed after being accused of shooting a police officer in 1989. Some have argued that Davis' case was nothing but a legalized lynching. Alluding to Davis' execution, is it not fair to say that other black and brown males could have been victims of racial injustice just like Davis had? Is it not a burden having to feel that your life, like that of Davis, as a black man could be taken away by a racially biased justice system against blacks and other minority groups? Is it not a burden to be afraid of being unfairly shot by police officers, like the cases of Amadou Diallo, Sean Bell, Oscar Grant, and Ramarley Graham, as well as by armed civilians, such as in the case of Trayvon Martin. These were five unarmed young black men murdered by New York police officers and a white civilian, respectively.

For university professors of color, is it not a burden having to constantly prove their intelligence to people who have questioned it? Is it not a burden having to constantly battle symbolic violence (Bourdieu, 1990, 1991, 1998)? Is it not a burden just thinking you could be denied employment and housing because of your skin tone? Finally, is it not a burden having to constantly prove to people who mistreat you that you are a human being just like them?

For people of color living, for example, in Africa and the Caribbean where there is a vast concentration of blacks, perhaps being black or brown, particularly for those who are privileged, may not feel like a burden, for they do not have to deal directly with the chronic forms of white supremacy and racism that many black and brown people have been experiencing in the United States, Europe, and Latin America. However, I argue that the negative and distorted images of black and brown people portrayed in the Western media and beyond are hurtful to all black and brown people, regardless of their geographical location. Moving from a country in which a person's blackness or brownness was not a concern to a country in which it is perceived and treated as something ugly and barbarous can make a person feel that being black or brown is a burden.

Let me restate that, by using the word *burden*, I have no intention to utilize a discourse of victimization to talk of the plight of black and brown people. Nor do I intend to blame all white people for the misery or educational and socioeconomic marginalization of black and brown people, because not all whites are racist exploiters, although all whites have benefited from institutional racism, which has automatically and historically favored them over people of color (Bonilla-Silva, 2010; Carr & Lund, 2007; Dei, 2009). This is why whiteness is one of the most heated topics and, as such, often comes to the forefront of political and educational debates revolving around inclusion, equity, and social justice.

Despite these words of caution, I am fully cognizant that what I articulate here might be interpreted by some as a self-defeating book written by an angry black man who hates whites. Instead of placing this label on me, I invite the reader to see this book as the deep expression of political, educational, and ideological positions of a black man who is courageous and has the audacity to affirm the humanity of black and brown people, including his own, in the face of a white world that has refused to see and treat people of color as equal to their white counterparts.

Moreover, although I do not intend to sound apologetic, I want to reiterate that my intention is not to create controversy with the content of this book. Rather, my goal is to articulate various challenges facing black and brown people in a white supremacist, linguicist, and racist world. The arguments I articulate illuminate the ways and degrees to which institutional racism, white supremacy along with "linguicism" (Phillipson, 2010) have affected the lives of black and brown people. This book points out the emotional and racial burdens black and brown people have experienced because of the unbearable weight of both overt and subtle forms of racism and linguicism they have been forced to carry in their lives within this white world.

Lastly, let me emphasize that, despite many similarities existing among black and brown people across the Atlantic, a person's experience as a black or brown person remains fundamentally unique because of the various factors mentioned earlier. This is to say that the experience of blacks from the Caribbean, for example, may not be the same as that of other blacks from Africa and other parts of the word. Their experience might also differ from the daily experience of African Americans, especially those who were born and grew up during the Jim Crow era, not to mention during slavery. However, I argue that all black and brown people around the globe have an inevitable reality confronting them that they cannot ignore: the burden having to face racism and white supremacy, which have limited their life chances.

No one has control over a person's race, native language, gender, and other identities in which the person is embodied. Therefore, no one should be discriminated against based on these characteristics. Unfortunately, because of feelings of hatred, bigotry, and fear of the "other," senseless crime has been committed against people who just happen to be different. In the case of black and brown people, fear of them circulated through the corporate media, schools, and churches has subjected them to many forms of oppression, racism among the worst. Fabricated fear circulated in the mainstream media and beyond about black and brown people, leading to their ill treatment, will not go away unless people of African descent and allies join their hearts, minds, souls, and spirits together to tirelessly fight against institutional racism, white supremacy, and other forms of oppression.

To Whom This Book Will Appeal

This book will hold appeal particularly to committed social justice educators, scholars, and community activists concerned with the racial, educational, linguistic, socioeconomic, and gender challenges facing black and brown people in the world. This book is also suitable to the needs of both graduate and undergraduate students interested in whiteness and blackness issues as well as postcolonial issues in education. Importantly, this book is relevant to the work of scholar activists and community organizers steadfastly committed to the betterment of human suffering and to the fight against various forms of oppression to which black and brown people and poor whites have been subjected.

Overview of Chapters

Chapter 1 examines the hegemonic nature of whiteness, which I call Whitecentricism and points out the ways it has influenced the lives of people of color. Chapter 1 ends by providing concrete proposals as to how whiteness can be de-centered, so all people can live in a racially inclusive society.

Chapter 2 explores the socio-economic, educational, and political conditions of black and brown people in the West, particularly in the United States. Specifically, Chapter 2 examines the ways and the degree to which institutional racism and the legacy of slavery continue to limit the life chances of black and brown people, including students, impacting their learning, their subjectivity, and their material conditions.

Chapter 3 examines whether democracy is possible in white male-dominated countries in which certain languages and cultures have been pushed to the margins, in which citizens are merely made spectators of educational, socio-economic, and political decision-making processes impacting their lives, and in which black, brown, and poor white workers have been disgustingly exploited. It begins by briefly discussing major tenets of democracy, deconstructing and challenging the Western definition of democracy. To further explore these tenets, it provides excerpts of a dialogue in which I engaged the world-renowned scholar and political dissident, Noam Chomsky, regarding democracy and schooling. It then examines the linguistic discrimination minority and racialized students have encountered and how these students have faced barriers in schools and in society at large. Chapter 3 concludes by making proposals as to what should be done so we can all live in a participatory form of democratic society in which the linguistic, educational, racial, socioeconomic, legal, political, and inalienable human rights of people, particularly racialized and marginalized groups, such as linguistically and culturally diverse students, are respected.

Chapter 4, using personal narratives as a form of inquiry, describes the learning experience of colonized subjects being educated in a colonial-based school system. It goes on to juxtapose such experiences with the challenge of teaching racialized, culturally, and linguistically diverse students in a standardized test-driven school context, such as that of the United States. In short, Chapter 4 critically examines the way and the extent to which the colonial legacy, combined with Western neocolonial and neoliberal policies, has continued to influence the teaching practices of teachers, as well as the learning of students both in the West and so-called "third world" countries, such as Haiti. Drawing on these experiences, I make suggestions as to how to counter neo-colonial and hegemonic practices affecting the learning, the well-being, and the teaching practices of both students and teachers.

Chapter 5 explicates the cultural, socio-economic, racial, and political factors that have shaped and reshaped the identities of black and brown people living in the US diaspora. Chapter 5 also describes the socio-economic and political circumstances that led to the migration of many people of color to the United States and the manner in which they have been experiencing racism, white supremacy, linguicism, and xenophobia.

Finally, the epilogue provides a deep and critical reflection on and analysis of the way the French colonial legacy, combined with Western neocolonial and neoliberal policies, influenced the teaching practices of teachers as well as the learning of students both in the West and in "third world" countries.

Final Thoughts

In writing this book, my deep hope is that readers will be inspired to fight against linguoracism, Whitecentricism, and related forms of oppression, regardless where these occur. Equally important, my sincere hope is that this book will add to the testimonies of people of African descent who have been victimized by, and have fought against, a racist system that is hostile to them. Only through constant struggles can we co-create a world in which a person's race, native language, social class, nationality, country of origin, and gender are not used as a pretext for mistreatment. Finally, we need to ensure that social constructs do not constitute obstacles that prevent people, namely racialized and marginalized groups, from having access to quality education, healthcare, decent jobs, a clean environment, and affordable and safe housing.

1

Whitecentricism Exposed:
De-centering Whiteness for a More Racially Inclusive Society

Introduction

Whiteness has been socially constructed as the standard of beauty, purity, innocence, and safety. As a result, whiteness has taken the center stage of attention through positive lenses. In contrast, what is associated with blackness or brownness is often represented as ugly, negative, and even dangerous. Drawing on the work of activist scholars, including white allies, who have written about and challenged white privileges (Dei, 2009; Wise, 2011) and autobiographical narratives, I critically examine whiteness as a dominant ideology structurally privileging whites over non-whites. I, then, go on to analyze the psychological and socio-economic effects of white dominance on People of Color. Finally, I propose that whiteness be de-centered for the construction of a more racially inclusive and equitable society.

Deconstructing Whiteness: An Overview

Despite that whiteness as an ideology is linked with the history of slavery, colonization, racism, and imperialism orchestrated by white European slave masters, colonizers, and white imperialist invaders and occupiers (Jensen, 2005; Lopez,

2005), it has been represented as "THE" standard of beauty, purity, innocence, and safety (Wise, 2011). Consequently, whiteness has taken the center stage of attention through positive lenses. On the contrary, blackness and brownness have been negatively constructed (Bonilla-Silva, 2003, 2010). Whiteness, as symbolically and ideologically represented, is something to which people, including historically marginalized and racialized groups, have been made to believe they should aspire. I call this widely and historically sold dominant ideology and innocent image of whiteness Whitecentricism, which consists of a set of hegemonic, discriminatory, and misleading practices of unfairly judging other races by the mythological representation of the so-called superiority of whiteness. Because this mythology about whiteness has been widely circulated and sold in schools, the media, and other institutions, there has historically been an inclination from individual whites to fiercely cling to a Whitecentric view of the world, however limited by those in power about such insight and understanding of other races and ethnicities. In other words, Whitecentric individuals tend to see the whole universe through their limited knowledge and understanding of other races and ethnicities. Convinced their white race is superior, they often look down on and mistreat people of different races, ethnicities, and cultures, particularly those belonging to lower classes, speaking languages that have been looked down on. Whitecentric individuals have tried to impose their norms, manners, styles of living, Western values, and habits on people from different races, ethnicities, and cultures, as if theirs are better than others'. In short, Whitecentric individuals have judged people by their own white standard widely sold as "THE" standard to look up to.

The ideology informing Whitecentricism has been challenged by many scholars (Carr & Lund, 2007; Carr, 2007; Dei, 2009b; Jensen, 2005; Leonardo, 2009; Kendall, 2012; McIntosh, 1992; Wise, 2011). However, the impact of such an ideology on people's consciousness, attitude, and actions is so pervasive that a person might rightfully ask whether the world is centered around whiteness. Many colonized and racially oppressed groups, as a result of internalized oppression, have unfortunately contributed to the hegemony and normalization of Whitecentricism by trying to look or act white (McNamara and O'Connor, 2006; Tyson, 2011).

This is often expressed and translated in their actions and attitudes. A prime example is women of African descent who have used wigs to make their hair look longer and straighter (Dillard, 2012). In the minds of many of these women, their natural hair, often labeled "afro hair," is not attractive enough and, therefore, has to be straightened to meet white standards, which hypothetically would enable them to fit into the white world. Research shows that millions of women of African descent have spent hundreds of dollars on hair extensions and on straightening their natural afro hair (Byrd & Tharps, 2001; Dillard, 2012; hooks, 1992a, 1992b; Stilson, 2009) to meet these standards. The few who have resisted this form of colonial mentality by maintaining their natural afro hair have been criticized and even ostracized by many black women, as well as black men (Dillard, 2006a, 2012; Stilson, 2009). Rarely have we seen, in major Hollywood movies, black women with their natural afro hair. The hair of black female actors usually looks straight. Likewise, the hair of black female hostesses of mainstream TV shows usually looks straight. Oprah Winfrey's hair is a prime example. Her hair is represented as straight in addition to the white, European attire that she often wears. The controversy around the 16-year-old African American, Gabby Douglas, is another case in point. Gabby was harshly criticized by many African Americans, particularly African American females, for keeping her afro hair natural while participating in the 2012 Olympics.

Very few female African American singers have kept their hair natural as well. The majority have either used wigs to make their hair appear long like that of white people's hair, or they have straightened it to accomplish the same goal. Worse yet, many African American women in music have colored their hair blond, like the iconic R&B singer, Beyonce. All of these superficial emulations have contributed to place and maintain whiteness at the center of attention, while pushing blackness and brownness to the margins. This is a colonial mentality that needs to be challenged and even eradicated. Both the Negritude movement and the Black Panther party tried to help people of African descent embrace, appreciate, and value black beauty through scholarly work, activism, and popular slogans, such as "I'm black, and I'm proud." One of the prominent female figures of the Black Panther Party, Angela Davis, proudly kept her afro hair natural, which has been an inspiration for many women of African descent (Dillard, 2012). Dillard states:

> By the mid-1970s, my hair was saying something else, itself singing the Black anthem of the times: "Say it loud. I am black, and I am proud!" Angela Davis had become my role model. Black had become my favorite color (even though my mother said that girls shouldn't wear "that" color: Pastels were so much more "appropriate"). So, while I couldn't wear the color black, I made up for it with Angela-wannabe hoop earrings that I bought with my own money from my retail sales job at the mall. And as the emerging sense of Black identity was coming into consciousness on my head, there was a little spark of Black consciousness rising inside me, too. (p. 31)

Despite the legacy of both the Negritude Movement and the Black Panther Party as well as their influences on people of African descent, many young and older blacks have been brainwashed by colonial and white hegemony discourses circulated in the mainstream media and schools to emulate whiteness by relaxing their hair. Dillard (2012) shares this form of internalized oppression in her personal narrative:

> But by the end of the 1970s, times weren't the only thing that changed. Chemically relaxed and permed hair, the kind that mimicked (often poorly) the Farrah Fawcett image on *Charlie's Angels* was the prevailing hairdo. And given the naps that the Lord had blessed me with, I had to work very hard to emulate this style. And it wasn't just the hair that I was working to get: It was all the accoutrements of Whiteness that went with it. My wish? "If I could say words the way they (White people)) say them. And while their language was never as alive in my ears as the Black speech was at home, that did not hamper my desire to acquire its "proper" cadence and sound. (p. 32)

White people's straight hair is not the only thing many black and brown people have tried to imitate. White skin, or something close to it, has been something many people of color, including Asians, have aspired to and, therefore, have tried to emulate. In their tireless effort to look white, many people of color have used special creams and soaps and chemical products, such as bleaches, to lighten their skin, whereas others have married whites with the hope that their children will have lighter complexions (Orelus, 2007). Products to lighten or whiten black or brown skin have been sold in many stores, particularly in beauty stores owned by people of African descent and Asians. On the packaging of these chemically based products, the images of fair skinned or white people are overwhelmingly represented as a way to convince and attract black or brown people to purchase these products. In a Sunday *New York Times* article, Thomas Fuller (2006) talks about the widespread skin-whitening products in Asia. Specifically, he argues that many Asians are determined to whiten their skin as a way to feel closer to becoming whites. Skin whitening has a long history in Asia, stemming from ancient China and Japan, where the saying "one white covers up three ugliness" was passed through the generations.

According to Fuller, these women have used special creams and soaps to whiten their skin. He went on to argue that, for these Asian women, looking white would guarantee them a good-paying job. Some institutions favor white-looking Asians in the hiring process. These women have whitened their skin to a point at which they have started developing skin problems. Fuller (2006) states:

Whiter skin is being aggressively marketed across Asia, with vast selections of skin-whitening creams on supermarket and pharmacy shelves testament to an industry that has flourished over the past decade. In Hong Kong, Malaysia, the Philippines, South Korea and Taiwan, 4 of every 10 women use a whitening cream, a survey by Synovate, a market research company, found. The skin-whitening craze is not just for the face. It includes creams that whiten darker patches of skin in armpits and "pink nipple" lotions that bleach away brown pigment. (p. 2)

My Memories of Whiteness and White Privileges

. . . racial/cultural memories can be thought of as memories of events as cultural beings that are/were so remarkable that we consider them to be defining moments in our life histories. . . . Pertaining to the latter, race/cultural memories are those related to our cultural identities that are so potent [often painful] that we tend to suppress [them] in order to function as human beings. (Husband, 2007, p. 10)

Our memories are based in a sense of connective and collective time, from which we both recognize our identities and from which we can also transform those identities. (Dillard, 2012, p. 9)

In this section, I select autoethnography as a medium of inquiry to reflect on my early memory of, and critically analyze through a postcolonial lens my experience with, whiteness and the privileges attached to it. I do so because autoethnography is personal yet political, historical and social (Holman Jones, 2005). It is composed of "research, writing, and methods that connect the autobiographical and personal to the cultural and social (Ellis, 2004, p. xix). Further, this form of self-reflexive inquiry allows me to challenge the "negation of the unrecognized accounts of the postcolonial subject" (Lavia, 2006, p. 189). Finally, I use autoethnography because it brings to the forefront the often silenced and undocumented narratives and lived experience of the marginalized, providing them a socio-historical space to come to voice (Alexander, 2005). In light of this view, I draw on and analyze critical moments that best reflect my lived experience as a colonized subject bearing witness to white dominance and privileges in a neocolonized land, Haiti, and Latin American countries, namely Colombia and Venezuela.

"*Ou se yon blan gason* [you're a white man]." This was the common sentence I grew up hearing. In the context of Haiti, when someone, particularly a black or a brown person, shows some level of generosity and kindness toward others, this person is automatically labeled a "*blan gason.*" The underlying meaning of this expression is that anything that is good is associated with being white. The reverse of this is that anything that is not good is attributed to its being black. So, growing up, I believed whiteness was the standard to look up to, and I was brainwashed to internalize this as a child. How could I not believe this Whitecentric myth? Whites from the United States who came to my neighborhood as missionaries were venerated and treated as if they were far superior to anybody else. Witnessing the first-class treatment they were receiving in my neighborhood, I envied them and wanted to look like them, because, as a native, I did not receive such treatment.

As a young boy, not yet able to understand the myth hidden behind whiteness and white skin privileges, I assumed people in my neighborhood were simply being hospitable to these white missionaries and visitors. I did not discover there was more to this than hospitality until I got older. The young adult Haitian males who were more or less advanced academically spent days practicing a song written in English and had high school students sing it to these white missionaries in a Christian church as a way to welcome them. Many Haitian women used creams to lighten their skin, apparently with the false hope that this would make them look more attractive to these white missionaries. They prepared and cooked the finest Haitian dishes for them, while these missionaries were sleeping with their teenage daughters, nieces, and other young girls in the neighborhood. Worse, some Haitian parents knew their teenage daughters were being raped by the so-called white Christians, but they did not take any action to stop such criminal acts.

It was revealed that many Haitian parents wished their daughters would get pregnant by white male missionaries, hoping this would bring a light-skinned child into the family. Moreover, it was not a secret to the public that the same white Christian missionaries had forced a lot of young Haitian girls to abort their children while the missionaries continued to date more than one girl at the same time. Ironically, these men were still getting the same respect they received when they first invaded our neighborhood. No castle or mansion could be built for them in this impoverished neighborhood, but the place they stayed had whatever they wanted: absolute respect, young girls, sexual gratification, fine Haitian food, and music. From what I observed, the behavior displayed, the actions taken, and the life style these white missionaries had in the island were no different from those of the French colonizers in Algeria, Congo, and Tunisia I learned about by exploring colonial and postcolonial literature, nor were they different from the Portuguese colonizers in Cape Verde and Mozambique; the British colonizers in Jamaica, Kenya, and Nigeria; or the Spaniards in South and Central America and Mexico during colonization.

These white men seized Haitian women from the Haitian men and enjoyed the finest food that many Haitians could not enjoy in their own land. In a word, they monopolized everything in the name of their whiteness and, before leaving our native land, they left the native people with a Bible, written by European white males, of which the content could not help these same people liberate themselves from mental slavery, white neo-colonial exploitation, the myth sealed in the white skin, and their miserable material conditions. Instead, with this Bible, the white missionaries simply taught us to pray, forgive, and love our enemies, but nothing about standing up to fight for our inalienable rights and to change our social and economic conditions. They taught us to keep hoping for a better life in heaven, whereas on earth we were starving and oppressed. From this painful experience with the white American evangelical missionaries, I concluded that the Bible did us no good but preached submissiveness and the art of ignorance to us.

With regard to the whitening cream noted previously, it is worth asking the following question: Who would have thought Haitians, descendants of Africans enslaved by the white French colonizers, would want to be closer in their skin tone to their colonizers after independence? Although many are aware and conscious of the negative effects of slavery on people of African descent, these same black and brown people have been brainwashed to believe they must mimic white people by lightening their skin to see themselves through a positive lens. This illustrates the extent to which the deep psychological effects slavery and colonization continue to have on people of African descent.

Despite various forms of oppression the slaves suffered from white slave masters and colonizers, many house slaves wanted to imitate and be like their white oppressors. Similar forms of internalized oppression have occurred in the so-called post-colonial and post-slavery eras. For example, although white supremacist and racist groups have been oppressive to black and brown people, many still want to emulate these groups physically by relaxing their hair and lightening their skin, not to mention that many have had operations to make their noses look like white peoples' noses. This is a social and historical phenomenon many people have yet to fully understand. Personally, I am still puzzled by the manner in which black and brown people want to be closer to whites in physical appearance as well as in attitude.

I also witnessed the role white privileges played in the interaction between whites and people of color in Latin America. While traveling with some white American and European friends, I personally witnessed the undivided attention they received from people, particularly women. For example, during the month I spent sharing an apartment with a Norwegian friend in Cartagena, Colombia, I was saddened to witness how much attention my 41-year-old friend received from

Colombian women and men. They treated him as if he were a king, while paying little attention to me. I was invisible in the eyes of many. For example, street vendors went straight to my friend, asking him to buy gifts, while ignoring me even though I was sitting next to him. Most of the local folks showed little interest in initiating conversation with me. However, my Norwegian friend felt overwhelmed by both male and female Colombians who wanted to hang out with him and show him places.

Likewise, in Maracay, Venezuela, I experienced a similar level of invisibility from a 6-year-old girl, who could be easily labeled a black girl based on her skin complexion. While attending a family gathering with my wife and some friends, this girl, who was leaving, kissed everybody goodbye except me. I was sitting next to my white, American, and Norwegian friends, and she jumped on and kissed all of them but skipped me. When my wife, my mother-in-law, and her own parents, out of embarrassment, asked this girl why she did not kiss me, she replied saying, "*A mi no me gusta a los negros*" (I do not like black people).

I was stunned to hear this black girl make such a statement. This experience once more made me realize that a person's blackness is on trial, regardless of where that person happens to be, whereas a person's whiteness is often cherished and venerated. From the many forms of invisibility that I have witnessed many blacks, including myself, experience in the United States and in Latin America, I have concluded that, in the colonized mind of many people, including people of African descent, white skin seems to symbolize prestige, beauty, and purity, whereas black skin represents ugliness, shame, and impurity—one of the consequences of the legacy of slavery and colonization.

Beyond Whitecentricism

Given the hegemonic influence of Whitecentricism, it is worth asking the following questions: Do black and brown people belong to the Western world, which has been so hostile to many of them? Where is their place in this world? Should they move back to Africa and join African brothers and sisters in their struggle against Western imperialism, neocolonialism, and political corruption in which many African political leaders and the national bourgeoisie have been involved? Or should they continue to live in the West and build alliances with other marginalized groups and white allies to fight against institutional racism and white supremacy? These are the questions that have preoccupied my mind and to which I have yet to find a clear answer. Going back to Africa is certainly an option, for this is the place where they originated.

However, moving back to Africa might not be the most viable solution, given the dire socio-economic and political situations of the continent caused by both western imperialism and internal political corruption (Dei, 2012). Furthermore, moving to Africa is not realistic for the following reasons: (1) As much as black and brown people want to idealize Africa, the fact remains it is not a homogenous continent (Dei, 2012). There is a mosaic of cultures and histories shaping this continent that many black and brown people as well as white people living in the West might not fully understand (Dei, 2012). As Dei states,

> Africa is complex, nuanced, and heterogeneous. Such acknowledgement of difference is key to appreciating the many challenges that confront the continent. It brings to the fore the fact that one-size solution offered to Africa's problems woefully lacks a depth of knowledge about the complexities of modern-day Africa. To begin to understand, teach, and learn about Africa, educators and students must understand Africa as more than a geographical space or territory. Africa is a place rich in culture and heritage, histories of struggles, successes, failures, and opportunities for moving ahead. (xix–xxi)

And (2) the fact that black and brown people living in the West are, in fact, black or brown does not necessarily mean they will be welcome. In fact, because many have been residing in the West, including the United States, and have been formally educated in the West, Africans might see and treat them as strangers, despite their historical and cultural African roots. In the eyes of some Africans living on the continent all their lives, many black and brown people would simply be just Westerners with black or brown faces.

Hence, the most realistic and practical option for many might be to continue to live in the West, which has become home to many. After all, to paraphrase Cabral (1973); Abdi (2005); Asante (2011); Fanon (1963); Dei (2012), and Said (1978), among others, what is called the Western world is essentially made of the exploited resources from the so-called "third world." In other words, the West, as we know it today, was built and continues to be built on the backbones and blood of black and brown people who were enslaved and colonized, many of whom have been marginalized since (Dei, 2012; Rodney, 1972). Through slavery and colonization, the West has enriched itself at the expense of black and brown people's labor and misery. Since slavery, people of African descent, through voluntary and involuntary migration (Ogbu, 1997), have enriched the West with their labor and the various cultures they brought with them. Thus, it can be rightfully argued that black and brown people, including myself, regardless of their country of origin, nationality, culture, language, and religion, have the right to be in the West, despite its hostility to them. What would the West have become without the labor of black and brown people? This question is subject to public and institutional debate. But I argue the West would have been totally different.

Previous generations of People of Color vigorously fought so that present and future generations of black and brown people could more or less have a voice and retain the right to exist. Because of our contribution to the socio-economic advancement of the West, particularly in the United States, I argue that we belong here, despite many of us having constantly faced Whitecentricism along with institutional racism. This sense of belonging has given many black and brown people, including myself, the strength to continue to fight for a better life not merely for themselves, but also for other racialized and marginalized groups. However, feeling that we rightfully belong to this land does not necessarily mean we are so naïve to believe we will be treated the same as our white counterparts, especially those who are privileged. Being born black or brown has much to do with the kind of treatment many black and brown people have received in this white world. In most cases, it has been ill treatment. Nonetheless, this sense of belonging challenges many to fight against racial, economic, and social injustice so the West can feel and be livable for everyone, not merely to those who have benefited from their class, white privileges, and other forms of privilege.

The journey of black and brown people in the Western world has been a long one, regardless of their social status as lawyers, university professors, or other highly regarded professionals. This is due to Whitecentricism, institutional racism, alongside the legacy of slavery and colonization. Although many have refused to allow themselves to be entrapped by this legacy, their daily experiences with racism and other forms of bigotry have made them cognizant of its harmful effects. It seems impossible to escape such a legacy. In short, because of the history of slavery and colonization, the racial identity of black and brown people has become a marker and has, therefore, made them a target. By saying this, I do not suggest that black and brown people should be sealed in the past, but, by the same token, black and brown people cannot pretend they are exempt from institutional racism and other forms of oppression simply because slavery and colonization are supposedly over. Pretense cannot and will never allow them to live a dignified life, nor can it enable them to find strength in their inner self to continue to fight against the racial war that has been launched against many of them and other marginalized groups. Pretense can only permit people to live a life of denial and lies.

Black and brown people should make an effort to transcend the history of colonization and slavery. However, this would require a lot of consistent effort because colonial stereotypes and prejudice continue to negatively impact them. Moreover, to rise above such a history, whiteness would need to be de-centered. That is, the political and socio-economic system that has historically placed whiteness at the center and has benefited whites, particularly elite whites, over people of color, needs to be restructured and reconfigured, so that everyone can inclusively have equal access to adequate resources to fulfill their potential, regardless of racial, ethnic, linguistic, and social backgrounds. Unless these *sine qua non* conditions are met, concepts such as social justice, equity, democracy, diversity, and freedom are nothing but empty rhetorics.

In other words, the materialization and the application of these concepts entail, first and foremost, a profound shift in the Western racial, socioeconomic, and political paradigms that have been instituted to favor certain groups of people who, by virtue of their race and class, have monopolized the wealth of the world. It is high time that the wealth accumulation by those who have historically been privileged is not continued at the expense of those with brown, black, and dark skin, which elite groups have used as a pretext to brutally exploit them.

Although slavery has been abolished for more 200 years ago, yet billions of people of African descent continue to suffer the most savage form of exploitation because of this sordid historical legacy maintained through white supremacy's ideology and practices. *Whitecentricism* should not be challenged through physical attacks and aggressive violence but rather through a complete transformation of the white ideological system that has been put in place to make Whites believe that they are superior to people from different races, ethnicities, and cultures. Such a situation is nothing but a decaying system, which should not exist anymore.

Conclusion

People who have benefited from this system should re-examine their consciences as human beings. Someone with a heart, who is endowed with human compassion and respect for his or her fellow human beings, should not tolerate the injustice inflicted on people who happen to be from different races, ethnicities, and cultures. Those who remain silent while witnessing racial, economic, social, and linguistic injustice taking place in the name of Whitecentricism should feel ashamed of themselves. True human worth depends on the protection of the well-being of other fellow human beings. The problem, however, is that many racist individuals do not see black and brown people as human beings. In their racist minds, people of African descent are sub-humans, who only deserve to be treated like the wretched of the earth (Fanon, 1963). This white dominant ideology is at the root of many cruel actions taken by some whites against People of Color.

How can a person help this category of whites understand that the blood that runs through the veins of all human beings is the same color? Likewise, how can a person make white racist individuals understand that when a person dies, his or her own skin tone will not matter, but rather what that person leaves behind as a legacy? Moreover, how can a person help racist individuals or groups understand that hatred shown toward people of color can simply lead to inner war with themselves and, consequently, to their mental misery? Furthermore, how can a person make bigoted groups realize that race is a social construct used as a pretext to deny the humanity of certain groups? Finally, how can a person help racist groups understand that, at the end of the day, we are all human beings?

Despite all forms of bigotry and hatred that many black and brown people have endured, it is hoped that Whitecentricism, along with institutionalized racism, will be eradicated and that, one by one, racist individuals will open their hearts and souls to people of different races. I believe we should all show love and compassion to others. Otherwise, sooner or later, the human tree that binds us all together will stop growing; it will wither because of our opaque hearts and souls that refuse to open themselves to respect and honor racial diversity and inclusivity.

2

Being Black and Brown in a White World: Challenges and Possibilities

The problem of the twentieth century is the problem of the color line—the relation of the darker to the lighter races of men in Asia and Africa, in America and the islands of the sea. (Du Bois, 1995, p. 23)

To my reading and experience, Whiteness is never invisible to those who daily live the effects of White dominance. Many Whites may see their Whiteness, and yet they are able to deny the dominance associated with it. This denial is not unconscious, nor is it accidental; I believe it is deliberate. (Dei, as cited in Carr & Lund, 2007, p. ix)

Within the more narrow context of the United States, the fundamental of the twenty-first century is the problem of the "structural racism": the problem deeply entrenched patterns of socioeconomic and political inequality and accumulated disadvantage that are coded by race and color and are consistently justified in public and private discourses by racist stereotypes, white indifference, and the prison industrial complex (Marable, as cited in Rickford, 2011, p. 279).

There is nothing the matter with blacks. The problem is White Racism and it rests squarely on the laps of the white racism. The sooner the liberals realize this the better for us blacks. (Biko, 2007, p. 25)

It is unquestionable that the activism, sacrifice, and hard work of the civil rights leaders and white allies have enabled many black and brown people to vote and have access to socio-economic, educational, and political opportunities. As such, it can be argued that, had Martin Luther King, Jr., Malcolm X, Rosa Parks, Cesar Chavez, Dolores Huerta, Jesse Jackson, Angela Davis, Denis Bank, and others not dedicated their lives to fight against racial and socio-economic injustice to pave the political road for future generations of black and brown people, Barack Obama, for example, would not have emerged on the political scene the way he did. Countering this argument, however, a person might state that Obama's political victory was inevitable because of his charisma and racial hybridity.

Depending on a person's level of understanding and awareness about the plight of black and brown people, he or she might argue that black and brown people are better off today than they were 50 years ago, especially when remembering the Jim Crow era during which black and brown people were ruthlessly brutalized, particularly by white supremacist groups, such as the Ku Klux Klan. However, if a person critically analyzes the achievement gap between students of color and their white counterparts, the decline in incomes, and other forms of socio-economic inequality that black and brown people, including students, have been experiencing for the last several decades, he or she would realize that substantially nothing has changed for them (Alexander, 2010).

In light of this view, this chapter explores the socio-economic, educational, and political conditions of black and brown people. Specifically, it examines the degree to which and the manner in which institutional racism and the legacy of slavery continue to limit life chances, pushing millions to racial, educational, socio-economic, and political margins. It is worth pointing out that a deep analysis of the conditions of brown people like Asians and Native Americans is beyond the scope of this inquiry. This chapter primarily focuses on the life conditions of blacks, African Americans, and Latinos/as.

Are Black and Brown Still at the Bottom of the Socio-economic Ladder?

As has been historically documented, during colonization and slavery, black and brown people experienced brutal forms of racism, socio-economic exploitation, and cultural oppression; however, history has taught us that black and brown people were not the only people forced into slavery (Firmin, 2000). Firmin eloquently states, "The most superficial look into history teaches us that slavery has been a universal phenomenon that has existed in every country and in every race. There is not a single European people who has not known slavery at a certain stage in its history as a nation" (pp. 334–335). Firmin goes on to illustrate:

> The very word "slave" is a clear indication that Blacks are not the only people to have known the degrading yoke of slavery. The word slave has its origin in the word "Slav," which is a reminder that a notable segment of the White race did experience servitude. Throughout the Orient, one finds Black and White slaves . . . . In Western Europe, the institution by the Romans had the sanction of the law and remained part of the mores for quite a long time. Bristol, London, Lyon, and Rome each had a slave market where Whites bought their congeners and subjected them to the same regime they would later apply, but with a much more exquisite cruelty, to the Africans taken away from their native land thrown into a life of ignorance and utter abjection. (p. 335)

As Firmin points out, throughout European history, blacks were not the only group enslaved. However, there was a stark difference between the way white and black slaves were treated by their masters. This fundamental difference has much to do with the racial background of black and white slaves. It is worth noting that race, as it came to be conceived in the context of modern slavery in the Americas, has taken a new social, political, and ideological meaning embedded in social policies and legal practices (Alexander, 2010). In other words, unlike before, race may not seem to be the underlying cause leading to the lynching of blacks; however, despite the so-called post-racial era, race is still the root cause of ill treatment of black and brown people (Asante, 2011; Bonilla-Silva, 2003, 2010).

Born free in the world like their white counterparts, black and brown people were quickly removed through the slave trade and placed in a world that has been economically, educationally, and politically hostile to them (Asante, 2011). The racist structure of this world has been very oppressive for more than 400 years. Because of institutional racism, the majority of black and brown people have been deprived of adequate health care, decent jobs, and quality education (Bonilla-Silva, 2010; Mills, 1997). For instance, "It is not news that so many Chicana/o high school students attend schools with poor conditions. Nor is it uncommon to restrict Chicana/o students to remedial and vocational courses of study within high schools" (Yosso, 2006, p. 57). Yosso (2006) goes on to state, "Out of 100 Chicana and Chicano elementary school students, only 44 graduate high school" (p. 57).

Other scholars, such as Mills (1997), capture the sharp socio-economic gap between black and white people. In *The Racial Contract,* Mills reports:

Whereas in 1988 black households earned sixty-two cents for every dollar earned by white households, the comparative differential with regard to wealth is much greater and, arguably, provides a more realistically negative picture of the prospects for closing the racial gap. (pp. 37–38)

Along the same lines, Shierholz and Gould (2011), two researchers from the Economic Policy Institute, report more recent data:

The black household earning the median income is now bringing in $5,494 less than the median black household did 10 years ago (a drop of 14.6 percent) and the median Hispanic household is now bringing in $4,235 less than the median Hispanic household did 10 years ago (a drop of 10.1 percent). (p. 1)

Shierholz and Gould further note:

Non-Hispanic whites maintained far lower poverty rates than any other racial/ethnic group. Blacks were particularly hard-hit by increases in poverty from 2009 to 2010, increasing 1.6 percentage points to reach a rate of 27.4 percent. In 2010, over one-third of black children (39.1 percent) and Hispanic children (35.0 percent) were living in poverty. The poverty rate for families with children headed by single mothers hit 40.7 percent in 2010. Of the 7.0 million families living in poverty in 2010, 4.1 million of them were headed by a single mom. (p. 3)

Bonilla-Silva attributed this persistence in income inequality between whites and people of color to what he called "a new racism." Bonilla-Silva states, "Today a new racism has emerged that is more sophisticated and subtle than Jim Crow and yet is as effective as the old in maintaining the (contemporary) racial status quo" (as cited in Leonardo, 2005, p. 18). Income disparity between people of color and their white counterparts illustrates Bonilla-Silva's argument of new racism. The phrase "new racism" captures the subtle and overt brutal form of racism that black and brown people continue to experience here in the United States and beyond. Despite the educational, socio-economic, and political opportunities which some few People of Color, such as President Barack Obama and the two former U.S. Secretaries of State, Colin Powell and Condoleezza Rice, have had to succeed politically and economically (thanks to the Civil Rights Movement and others), the majority of black and brown people, including students, are still oppressed.

With regard to African Americans particularly, studies show their unemployment rate has persisted steadily during the last 50 years (Austin, 2012; Fairlie & Sundstrom, 1999). It is not surprising, therefore, due to institutional racism, that people of color, particularly African Americans, Native Americans, and Latinos/as, are still at the bottom of the well (Bell, 1992). For example, segregation, including school segregation, is a recurrent racial and socio-economic phenomenon that black and brown people face and, therefore, must be brought to the forefront of debates revolved around racial justice. Tatum (2007) states:

> As long as we live in residentially segregated neighborhoods, it seems we will inevitably have segregated public schools. The strategy of using transportation to achieve racial balance in schools was effective in many communities, particularly in the South, but not popular among community decision makers, as evidenced by the rapid return to neighborhood school assignments once judicial intervention was removed. (p. 16)

I argue that insofar neighborhoods and institutions, such as schools and the work place, are racially and ethnically segregated, black and brown people and whites will only have a superficial understanding of one another. True interracial and ethnic relations take place when people are integrated in schools that genuinely support racial, ethnic, and linguistic diversity. Schools' failure to do so has led many students to rely on the media to be "informed" about other ethnic and racial groups. Unfortunately, the media, for the most part, have portrayed a superficial and negative image of underprivileged racialized groups, such as blacks, Latinos/as, Asians, Native Americans, and Arabs. Tatum (2007) goes on to say:

> As school districts move back to neighborhood school policies, the next generation of White students will likely have less school contact with People of Color than their predecessors did. Particularly for young White children, interaction with People of Color is likely to be a virtual reality rather than an actual one, with media images (often negative ones) most clearly shaping their attitudes and perceived knowledge of communities of color. The progress that has been made in the reduction of racial prejudice that can be associated with shared school experiences is at risk of stalling. (p. 14)

The new racism that blacks and Latinos/as have been experiencing is somewhat reflected in the statistics that Shierholz and Gould and Austin provided above. Institutional racism has not only affected black and brown people economically and politically, but it has also played a role in their misrepresentation in the media and in the school curriculum. Through schooling and the media, people, including students, have internalized negative images portrayed about blacks and Latinos/as and other marginalized groups. I argue that institutionalized racism is the underlying cause of the irrational fear that some whites have about black and brown people, particularly black and brown men. For example, the case of Trayvon Martin and

Georges Zimmerman illustrates that many whites and even people of color are suspicious and fearful of black and brown men because of how they have been negatively portrayed in the mainstream media. Further, because of widely circulated stereotypes through the mainstream media, their presence in some white neighborhoods is often felt as a threat to many uninformed and racially prejudiced whites. These groups of whites are notorious for rushing to move out when a few black and brown people dare to move into their neighborhoods. This fear of black and brown people is not innocent; nor is it accidental. It is rooted in and learned from institutions, such as families, schools, and the mainstream media, to which I turn next.

The Role of the Media in Perpetuating Stereotypes about People of Color

Historically, the mass corporate media are known for projecting distinct images of black, brown, and white people. Blacks and Latinos/as, especially males, for example, have been grossly misrepresented in mainstream movies. Specifically, they have been portrayed as violent, as thieves, and as drug dealers. Through movies, the media have presented two different worlds: A People of Color world and a white world. The division of the two worlds is made so visible through the mass corporate media that it has been engrained in the minds of many whites and People of Color alike. Consequently, a great number of people believe that black and brown people, particularly black and brown men, are aggressive, are rapists, are stupid, or are just savage (Macedo & Steinberg, 2007). Ironically, there are also people of color who have internalized these stereotypes and negative images about black and brown men. The division between whites and people of color, particularly blacks, Latinos/as, and Native Americans, created and promoted by the corporate mass media has become, in some way, part of this nation's consciousness.

Because of this division, many white students and students of color, for example, tend to create their own little world in school cafeterias, segregating themselves as if they have nothing in common to share and enjoy between them (Tatum, 2003). Their interaction is often nonexistent or poor. Sometimes, they communicate or interact because they have an obligation to do so for matters related to sports or other activities. Otherwise, they do not willingly mingle. In fact, from both my personal and professional observation, black, brown, and white people might be colleagues, yet some white people do not invite their black and brown colleagues to their houses for dinner or social gatherings. I also know many black and brown people who do the same. These forms of separatist practices are problematic in the sense that they do not contribute to unity among whites and People of Color.

Whites fear People of Color, because they have been misrepresented through the mainstream media (Hall, 1997). Similarly, the US legal and political institutions have allowed whites to separate themselves from black and brown people. This has occurred through school segregation and housing discrimination, preventing black and brown people from attending the same schools and living in the same neighborhoods as some whites (Kozol, 2006; Tatum, 2007). However, widely circulated stereotypes about black and brown people do not deter racially prejudiced whites from enjoying the talent of black and brown athletes and artists (Zirin, 2009). Many might not have "a problem" with black and brown people as far as entertainment is concerned. In their living rooms or at the stadium, they watch basketball or football games, dominated by functionally literate or semi-literate black and brown players who toil to enrich privileged white male CEOs and owners of these football or basketball teams (Hutardo, 1996; Zirin, 2009). Hutardo (1996) notes,

> Ironically, although many professional sports are played by men of Color, these men are often not in the decision-making process positions of constructing them or in the organized rituals of watching them with those in power. The recent work on whiteness begins to document how the activities of participating in or watching ritualized sports are used to socialize individuals of privilege to the dynamics of power. The power that whiteness holds for its owners has not been explicitly documented (C.I. Harris, 1993a); it is a birthright that is socialized from generation to generation in the largely racially segregated living arrangements that exist in the United States (McIntosh, 1992, p. 77). (p. 146)

Likewise, many prejudiced whites might not find it inconvenient to have black and brown musicians or comedians perform for them in their neighborhoods, provided these black and brown musicians or comedians and their fans do not hang out there for too long after the performances are over. For many prejudiced whites, it is safer to be "informed" about black and brown people through the corporate mass media, in which the latter are misrepresented (Hall, 1997; Moore, 2001).

Given the extent to which black and brown people have been misrepresented, it is not surprising that many whites have mistrusted them. How can someone not be afraid of black and brown people when they are portrayed so negatively on TV, particularly through major Hollywood movies? How can someone not be reluctant to hire qualified black and brown people when they are portrayed as aggressive, lazy, and irresponsible? These stereotypes about black and brown people circulated through the mass corporate media have, unfortunately, been the main ideological and political tools that many prejudiced and economically and politically powerful whites have used to maintain the unequal socio-economic and political power relations between privileged whites, People of Color, and poor whites.

Generally, the white world sparkles like a diamond with the longest life expectancy and ample economic, educational, and political opportunities. Broadly speaking, the world of People of Color, conversely, is silently dying from a lack of educational and political opportunities coupled with a health care system that does not work for many of them. This form of racial inequality explains the underlying reasons that many blacks during slavery preferred to commit suicide rather than to live in a world in which their freedom was the property of their masters. In the post-slavery era and the so-called post-racial era, many black and brown people have continued to labor to maximize the corporate profits of those in power; however, for many, having two meals a day is a luxury and getting a decent job is a struggle, whereas, for others, completing a college degree is sometimes the product of luck or a scholarship.

Black and brown people have continued to be marginalized in a society that has refused to treat them equally. Because of institutional racism, black and brown people have been the first to be attacked by police officers on the street and to be denied quality education, decent jobs, and housing. Black and brown children have been locked up in a school system that is structurally designed to fail them rather than prepare them to succeed in life. Macedo (1994), who captures this racial injustice, maintains, "It is the same colonial model that fails most of the subordinate students in urban schools" (p. 81). Similarly, Kozol (1991), in *Savage Inequalities*, eloquently described the neo-colonized conditions in which poor black kids were expected to "learn":

> In schools with an all-white student body, the average ran up to $350 allocated per pupil per year. In three heavily Negro districts, by comparison, the averages were $240, $235, and $232. In-class expenditures for Boston as a whole averaged $275 per pupil. In the Negro schools: $213. It was apparent from this report that Negro areas also had the highest percentage of provisional teachers, those who were fill-ins, and no tenure, no seniority, no experience, and no obligation to remain. These seem amazing facts in a country, which daydreams about exporting its democracy. Looking at these figures openly, it is hard not to wonder whether we did not export our democracy a long time ago and now do not have very much of it left for our own people. It is certain that we do not have a great deal of it to spare for the Negro. (p. 56)

The savage inequality that Kozol describes in his book is dated more than 20 years ago. However, inequities still exist at even far higher figures. As a former high school teacher teaching in an underfunded school located in the most marginalized neighborhood in Boston, Massachusetts, I can speak to some of what Kozol points out. I remember how frustrated I became when I did not have adequate resources to teach my minority students, including English language learners of color. Through their eyes and attitude, they vividly expressed the greatest desire and passion to learn, but how could I offer them the education they deserved when school materials were scarce and I shared a tiny classroom with broken windows with another teacher? How could they concentrate when they came to my class hungry and told me that their parents did not have money to buy school supplies?

Black and brown people whose social class has enabled them to get an education and be successful despite the institutionalization of racism have still been subject to both overt and subtle racism. For instance, although Cornel West (1993) is a well-known and highly respected scholar, his fame and scholarship did not exempt him from the same ugly racist treatment by white police officers that ordinary black and brown people experience in their daily lives. West narrates his experience:

> Years ago, while driving from New York to teach at Williams College, I was stopped on fake charges of trafficking cocaine. When I told the police officer I was a professor of religion, he replied, "Yeh, and I'm the Flying Nun. Let's go, nigger!" I was stopped three times in my first ten days in Princeton for driving too slowly on a residential street with a speed limit of twenty-five miles per hour. (p. xi)

As West's testimony illustrates, the racial oppression inflicted on black and brown people during colonization and slavery has taken a different form through racial profiling and symbolic violence (Bourdieu, 1990). Ryan (1976) argues:

> As the murderer pleads guilty to manslaughter to avoid a conviction that might lead to his being electrocuted, liberal America today is pleading guilty to savagery and oppression against the Negro of one hundred years ago in order to escape trial for the crimes of today. (p. 51)

Another form of racial injustice worth pointing out is that black and brown people are expected to pay the price for any action that an individual black or brown person commits. That is, if a black or brown person commits a crime, it is often assumed that all black or brown people are violent.

However, when a white person kills a black person or white soldiers mistreat and dehumanize prisoners of a different race, religion, and color, as has happened in the United States' detainment camp in Guantanamo Bay, Cuba, and in Abu Ghraib, Iraq, the mass corporate media present this criminal act as an individual act committed by socially deviant white persons or soldiers. The cruel acts committed by white people, such as Timothy McVeigh, who killed many innocent people by bombing the federal building in Oklahoma City, and the US soldiers in Iraq and Guantanamo Bay, who humiliated and tortured many innocent people who looked different and professed the religion of Islam, have not consequently subjected all white Americans to racial profiling and stigma. The racial stereotypes and stigma against black and brown people have much to do with institutional racism supported by institutions, such as schools and the mainstream media. Those in power often blame racially marginalized groups for their miserable socio-economic conditions, failing to point out that racism, along with classism, is the root cause of these conditions.

Like whites, black and brown people can achieve great things and succeed in life if given the opportunity. However, because of unequal distribution of resources and opportunity gaps, many People of Color, including linguistically and culturally diverse students, have not been as successful academically and economically as whites. Is this a historical coincidence or conspiracy? I argue that the striking difference between whites and People of Color is intrinsically linked to institutional racism and an inequitable distribution of resources. Prejudiced powerful whites have used the mainstream corporate media to portray black and brown people as inferior, stupid, savage, uncivilized, and lazy so they could justify their monopolization of the wealth of the earth. Black and brown people have been allowed to pick up the crumbs of the wealth of the world because of institutional racism leading to their racial and socio-economic marginalization.

Although many people of African descent have contributed to the scientific advancement of the Western world, they have not been acknowledged enough in Western history textbooks for their contribution (Asante, 2011; Loewen, 1995; Teresi, 2002). Instead, in many instances, they have been victims of Western scientific inventions. For example, the electrical machine that the US legal system has used to unjustly electrocute many young black and brown men and women was not invented by People of Color. Moreover, the dangerous weapons used to kill Patrice Lumumba in Congo, Steve Biko in South Africa, Thomas Sankara in Burkina Faso, and Malcolm X and Martin Luther King in the United States were not invented by black or brown people. Finally, the bombs the United States used to destroy Hiroshima, killing thousands of innocent Japanese children and elderly and has continued to be used to kill innocent people in countries, such as Iraq, Afghanistan, and Pakistan, were not invented by black or brown people.

However, because of the ugly images the mainstream media have projected of black and brown people, their skin pigmentation has been "a marker" throughout the world. In other words, their skin color, which has been unjustly associated with violence, robbery, and laziness, constitutes a shadow that follows black and brown people from adolescence through adulthood. Therefore, it comes as no surprise that black and brown people have been denied many opportunities and are, in most cases, the first to be racially profiled and killed on the streets in New York and Los Angeles by prejudiced police officers. In short, because of their blackness and brownness, their life seems to be always on trial.

Black and brown people not only have to prove themselves as capable human beings, but also as capable black and brown beings, as they are usually seen and treated as a double creature—a racial and socio-political phenomenon that Du Bois (1995) called double consciousness. First, they are perceived and treated as blacks and browns. After they prove themselves as "good citizens," they are sometimes treated as human beings. Because of institutional racism and the legacy of racism, black and brown people have been perceived and often treated as subhuman (Bonilla-Silva, 2010; Fanon, 1967; Orelus, 2011a). Consequently, many have been denied the opportunity to fulfill their potential. To compensate for their "incompleteness," as socially constructed by the white world, black and brown people are generally expected to be either obedient and extremely nice or feel they have to outperform their white counterparts to receive the respect they deserve. Because of racial prejudice and stereotypes, in such fields as sports in which they have been given a chance to participate, black and brown people are expected to outperform their white teammates. Those who do not succeed in passing the white world test are usually perceived and treated as failures, as inferior, useless, and dirty, lazy blacks. Fanon (1967) stated, "There is a fact: whites consider themselves superior to black men. There is another fact: Black men want to prove to white men, at all costs, the richness of their thought, the equal value of their intellect" (p. 10).

Given the deplorable racial and socioeconomic situations that black and brown people have been forced into, I ask whether or not they will be able to transcend these situations and succeed? I further ask: Can they go beyond negative images and stereotypes that have been constructed about them since slavery and still succeed? I remain convinced they can. To be successful, black and brown people need to steadily cherish their culture, explore further, and hold onto their rich historical legacy and cultural traditions, which have been negated by those in power who strive to maintain white hegemony. Otherwise, they will be condemned to living up to the white world's standard. Césaire (2000) states:

> We lived in an atmosphere of rejection, and we developed an inferiority complex. I have always thought that the black man was searching for his identity. And it has seemed to me that if we want to establish this identity, then we must have a concrete consciousness of what we are, that is, of the first fact of our lives: that we are black; that we were black and have a history, a history that contains cultural elements of great value; and that Negroes were not, as you put it, born yesterday, because there have been beautiful and important black civilizations. (pp. 91–92)

Because of a white racial superiority discourse circulated through textbooks and the mainstream media, many white people have learned to believe they have a biological right to lead the world, to control and oppress blacks, browns, and other marginalized people. To counter such a racist and white hegemonic ideology, it is imperative that black and brown people use historical facts to remind the ignorant, the arrogant, and the racist whites that they have gotten it wrong. Black and brown people can begin by using a simple historical fact that has proven the grandeur, high intelligence, and strong skills of black people: The Egyptian civilization. No one, not even the coldest and most inhuman racist people on earth can question and doubt the beauty and the splendid legacy of this great civilization (Diop, 1974).

It is, therefore, worth asking: What do racist Americans and Europeans, such as Jensen (1969), Herrnstein and Murray (1996), and Gobineau (2010) have to say about the great pyramids built in Egypt without the sophisticated technology to which Europeans and white Americans have had access? Does one need to teach them world history, which great black and brown heroes, heroines, and critical thinkers, such as Sojourner Truth, Rosa Parks, Cesar Chavez, Toussaint L'Ouverture, Simon Bolivar, W.E.B Du Bois, Amilcar Cabral, Dolores Huerta, Steve Biko, Malcolm X, Nelson Mandela, Yuri Kochiyama, Toni Morrison, Martin Luther King, Jr., Frederick Douglass, Antenor Firmin, Frantz Fanon, Aime Césaire, Jean Price Mars, and C.L.R. James, have shaped through splendid leadership skills and exceptional scholarly work? Black and brown people need to remind racist European and American scientists and writers about the historical and cultural significance of the Egyptian civilization (Diop, 1974; Firmin, 2000). Firmin (2000) asserts:

> One of the surest ways to refute such a theory (i.e., the theory of inequality of human races) would be to identify a period in history when the proud Europeans were absolutely savages while Black people were holding up the flame of early civ-

ilization. Let us open the annals of humanity and question the past. Let us study the vestiges of antiquity, for they have much to teach us and they can shed much light on the debate and confirm the truth. At the dawn of history we encounter one people whose civilization precedes all the others: the ancient population of Egypt. These people, who were unquestionably the initiators of the White nations of the West in science and the arts, had created alone, on the shores of the Nile whose sandy sweet waters flow across such vast lands, the most impressive social organization that a human population had ever built. (p. 226)

World History needs to be taught in schools from the perspective of the oppressed so black and brown people and other marginalized people can have access to the historical facts to which Firmin refers. Unless this happens, marginalized black and brown people will continue to be duped, lied to, and misled and, consequently, will naïvely accept the fairytale version of the history white dominant conservative groups have been selling them through institutions such as schools and the media. Worse, they will continue to be brainwashed into believing that white, straight, Christian, able-bodied, privileged men were born to rule the world and others were destined to be their subalterns.

The exploitation of black and brown people and other subjugated groups does not happen in a vacuum; it has been well orchestrated through two oppressive joint systems, capitalism and racism, which I would call the twins of inequalities. Racism is alienating, oppressive, and inhuman, yet the white, capitalist, dominant class has used it to maximize their profits by exploiting black and brown people. In other words, the white economic and political world has been built on the backbone of black and brown people and other subordinate groups. That is, capitalists use racism to dehumanize and exploit people of color. I argued elsewhere (Orelus, 2009, 2011b) that one cannot truly understand racism without having a clear understanding of capitalism and vice versa. Black and brown people's skin tone has been used, in most cases, by white capitalists to justify the economic inequality that those black and brown people have experienced; the political and psychological violence they have endured; and the poverty that has crippled many of them. Simply put, racism has helped the white dominant class achieve its goal of oppression, exploitation, and exclusion. Moreover, by rationalizing racism and using it as a political and economic weapon to strengthen power, the prejudiced, white, upper-class has rendered alienation, oppression, and famine the *raison d'être* of People of Color.

What is to be done against these oppressive socio-economic and political situations? As Douglass (2012) reminds us, coercive power does not willingly free oppressed and marginalized groups until the latter show their firm determination to challenge and fight against this power to gain their freedom. For example, in South Africa, the apartheid system would still be in place to oppress and exploit the Africaners, had the latter not resolved to fight against this evil system. Moreover, the Haitian and Algerian people would still live under the terror, tyranny, inhuman exploitation, and oppression of their French colonizers, had they not rigorously fought against them. As the first step toward their freedom, I propose that black and brown people in the United States and beyond awaken and start asking themselves the following questions:

1. Is the social inequality black and brown people and other marginalized groups are facing the end result of their racial inferiority, or is it the capitalist and racist system that has denied them opportunities?
2. Are black and brown people poor because they are lazy or because of institutional racism and capitalism?
3. Are black and brown people unable to compete with whites because they are not as intelligent or smart or because they have been denied quality education that many whites, especially privileged whites, often take for granted?

The questions posed speak directly to the inhuman conditions black and brown people in the Americas and beyond have been forced to live in for centuries. Moreover, these questions unveil the lies that black and brown people have been told about their socio-economic and political situations. For example, the white dominant ideology circulated through institutions, such as the media, schools, and churches, is intended to make black and brown people believe their "biological inferiority" is the root cause of their sufferings and misery. Countering this argument, I contend that their inhuman socio-economic conditions are directly linked to both the capitalist and racist systems.

Conclusion

As this chapter demonstrates, millions continue to be victims of job discrimination and unemployment and are deprived quality education and healthcare. Economically, educationally, and politically, we have two worlds in front of us: a white world and a People of Color world. However, white and black politicians alike, including President Barack Obama, have used lofty political rhetoric to convince people there is no such thing as a black, Latino/a, Native American, and white America and that there is only the United States of America. However, the present socio-economic and educational inequalities between People of Color and whites suggest that, in fact, there is a black, a white, a Native American, and a Latino/a America, and these diverse racial groups are segregated. To bridge the educational and socio-economic gaps between whites and People of Color, especially those who are poor, I propose that black and brown people and white allies continue to organize and build stronger alliances to fight against institutional racism and corporate capitalism to create a better world for themselves, their children, and other people's children.

3

Reframing the Debate on Democratic, Educational, and Linguistic Rights of Minorities

The recognition of democracy as a site of struggle is significant to the issue of cultural democracy, where the struggle is focused specifically on the issue of culture and power and on who controls cultural truths. Unfortunately, democracy often has been reduced simplistically to an unqualified principle of majority rule, while minority groups are ignored as a part of the society at large. When this occurs—and consequently minority interests, views, and convictions are disregarded in the institutional process of decision-making, and certain groups are permanently relegated to a minority position—such a democracy is likely to become unstable and lose legitimacy in the eyes of its citizens. (Darder, 2011, p. 32)

American monolingualism is part and parcel of an assimilationist ideology that decimated the American indigenous languages as well as the many languages brought to this shore by various waves of immigrants. As the mainstream culture felt threatened by the presence of multiple languages, which were perceived as competing with English, the reaction by the media, educational institutions, and government agencies was to launch periodic assaults on languages other than English. (Macedo, Dendrinos, & Gounari, 2003, p. 23).

Is democracy possible in countries in which racialized, minoritized groups and their languages and cultures have been pushed to the margins; in which racially marginalized people are merely spectators of educational, socio-economic, and political decision-making processes affecting their lives; and in which workers, especially minority workers, have been grossly exploited? This chapter explores these questions. To this end, I begin by reviewing major tenets of democracy as related to schooling. To further examine these tenets, I use excerpts of a dialogue in which I engage the world-renowned scholar and political dissident, Noam Chomsky, about democracy and schooling. This dialogue is situated within the contemporary U.S. educational and neoliberal context, including the No Child Left Behind legislation. I explore linguistic discrimination against minority students and how these students have faced barriers in schools and in society at-large. This chapter concludes by making an appeal for linguistic and cultural diversity as one of those *sine qua non* conditions if we are to live in a participatory form of democracy.

Democracy: Whose Definition and Whose Interests Does It Serve?

At the outset, it is important to note that concepts, such as economic democracy, ecological democracy, and democracy in the social realm, which are important aspects of direct democracy, are beyond the scope of this chapter. Broadly conceived, the concept of democracy has been at the center of many political debates and can be traced back as far as the time of Plato. This concept occupied a central role in Plato's work, namely in his book, *The Republic* (Plato, 2008). However, despite the fact that *The Republic* is a groundbreaking text, it is well documented that Plato, rather than a supporter of a participatory form of democracy, was a supporter of oligarchy in which the government is ruled by the enlightened few (Baird & Kaufmann, 2008).

Many scholars from various fields and with different foci, including education, philosophy, and political science, have challenged Plato's view on democracy and developed a much more progressive view of this concept (Carr, 2011; Chomsky, 1994, 2007; Denzin, 2009; Dewey, 1997; Giroux, 2003, 2007; Macedo, 2009). For example, Dewey (1997), the prominent American philosopher and educator, was a champion of a democratic school system. Specifically, through his book, *Democracy and Education*, Dewey advocated for democratic educational values and principles, which he argued should be the cornerstone of any progressive society.

Furthermore, Dewey emphasized the great value and role of democracy in the construction of an equitable society. Moreover, he argued that embracing and implementing democratic values and principles in any given society can be conducive to the political stability of a country and the overall well-being of its citizens. In addition, unlike Plato, Dewey was against oligarchic and authoritarian forms of government often ruled by the wealthy at the expense of the poor (Greene, 2009).

With regard to schooling, in particular, Dewey advocated creating democratic space within the U.S. school system, for he believed that such a space was essential for the creation of good citizenship. Finally, Dewey believed that students and professors should be allowed to discuss social and political issues in schools without the intrusion and infringement of the government. In other words, Dewey believed that students' and professors' voices should not be silenced if democracy is to exist. As Maxine Greene (2009) eloquently put it, "Without a Dewey, there would have been little concern for 'participatory democracy,' for 'consensus,' for the reconstitution of a public sphere" (p. 92). I agree with Greene's view, although I would add that the United States is not the only country in which there have been debates around the meaning of "democracy."

Taking Dewey's view on democracy and schooling a few steps further, I argue that to have a democratic school system, students, particularly culturally and linguistically diverse students, need to be allowed to voice their opinion about what kind of education they feel they deserve to receive. Also, these students should be given the opportunity to actively participate in the co-construction of knowledge with their teachers (Orelus, 2010; Vygotsky, 1978). In my view, a school system within which students are expected to merely receive and regurgitate the information their teachers pass on to them is not democratic. As the Brazilian educator Paulo Freire (1993, 2005) pointed out in his seminal work, *Pedagogy of the Oppressed*, students should not be passive recipients of prefabricated knowledge professors pour into their heads. Freire called this form of pedagogy a "banking" form of education.

Freire's notion of a banking form of education is unfortunately not an obsolete form. It has been a recurring practice in the U.S. school system, especially with the passage of the No Child Left Behind mandate. Because of this neoliberal educational reform, many urban school teachers have been hard pressed to teach to the test with the hope that students would meet state and federal standardized test benchmarks (Linn, 2004; Lipman, 2004; Sleeter, 2005). Simply put, the neoliberal agenda informing this type of educational reform has essentially de-intellectualized teachers and led to the mis-education of students (Giroux, 2007; Orelus, 2010). That is, because of the neoliberal nature of this educational reform, the teaching practices of many public school teachers have been reduced to mostly rote and drill test practices, leaving limited space for creative and critical work conducive to student growth and learning (Lipman, 2004; Sleeter, 2005).

Schools and politics are not two separate entities. Therefore, what is happening in schools needs situated and configured within a country's political system. West (2004) and Chomsky (2007), among others, have been very critical of the U.S. political system and concur that, in a democratic society, people, including students and teachers, should assert their voices without fear of governmental repressive measures. These public intellectuals similarly argue that citizens should be allowed to actively participate in the political decision-making processes and that they should not merely be passive spectators of what happens. Critiquing the U.S. system of democracy, West (2004) states:

> The American democratic experiment is unique in human history not because we are God's chosen people to lead the world, nor because we are a force for good in the world, but because of our refusal to acknowledge the deeply racist and imperial roots of our democratic project. We are exceptional because of our denial of the antidemocratic foundation stones of American democracy. (p. 41)

In a country in which minority students, particularly bilingual students, have been forced to embrace and speak English at the expense of their native tongues (Cummins, 2000; Crawford, 2008; Macedo et al., 2003; Valdés, 2001; Valdés, Capitelli, & Alvarez, 2010), in which workers have been exploited and are put under surveillance causing them to revolt against their inhuman conditions (Aronowitz, 2006; McLaren, 2005), and in which students have often been rewarded for being silent and compliant (Giroux, 2003), the concept of democracy becomes more of an illusion than a reality. Furthermore, one is dissuaded from talking about a progressive form of democracy in a country in which a small group of wealthy people control the information circulated through TV, newspapers, and radio stations that they themselves own (Chomsky, 2002; Leistyna & Alper, 2007; Macedo & Steinberg, 2007). Likewise, there cannot be democracy without the equal and representative voices and active participation of all citizens in political decisions concerning and affecting their own lives. Moreover, democracy is an illusion in a capitalist, neoliberal state in which profits are the priority, not the people (Chomsky, 2004; Klein, 2007; McLaren, 2005, 2008; Porfilio and Malott, 2008). Finally, as Alexander (2010) documented in her book, *The New Jim Crow*, democracy has yet to become a reality for those, namely poor blacks and Latino/as, who are unjustly and massively incarcerated and have been treated as the "wretched of the earth" (Fanon, 1963) in the U.S. prison system.

Unfortunately, this democracy myth has been ingrained in the minds of many in many countries, including the United States, which has dubiously been called and refers to itself as the preeminent democratic country. Like Chomsky (2004) and West (2004), De Tocqueville (2000) and Myrdal (1944), decades earlier, already unveiled the contradictory nature of the U.S. political system. As these authors observed, although the United States has earned a democratic reputation worldwide, many groups, such as African Americans, Native Americans, Latino/as, and Arabs, among many others, have historically suffered brutal forms of discrimination, including racial profiling and linguistic discrimination.

For example, although the grand narrative about democracy continues to shape public discourse and circulate in the white mainstream media and schools, historically marginalized and racialized groups have been forbidden from speaking their languages. In fact, their languages have been attacked and relegated to an inferior status. Native American children, forcibly placed in reservations, were often reprimanded in government schools for speaking their native languages, perceived by their white teachers as "uncivilized" (Churchill, 2004; Grande, 2004; Spring, 2009). Likewise, in Australia, Aboriginal children were compulsorily taken from their families and placed in boarding schools in which they were prohibited from speaking their native tongue and their names were changed to Anglo names (Olsen, 2003).

In his seminal book, *How Europe Underdeveloped Africa*, Walter Rodney (1972) documented the way and the extent to which European colonizers imposed their languages on African children to maintain their linguistic, political, and socioeconomic domination. According to Rodney, to achieve this goal, the European colonizers hired submissive teachers to teach African students European culture and history in kindergarten and primary schools. Through this colonial form of schooling, African students were taught to value and embrace the language and culture of their colonizers at the expense of their own. Rodney states:

> Schools of kindergarten and primary level for Africans in Portuguese colonies were nothing but agencies for the spread of the Portuguese language. Most schools were controlled by the Catholic Church, as a reflection of the unity of church and state in fascist Portugal. In the little-known Spanish colony of Guinea (Rio Muni), the small amount of education given to Africans was based on eliminating the use of local languages by the pupils and on instilling in their hearts the holy fear of God. (p. 249)

Finally, in the United States, other marginalized groups, such as Latinos/as have been prohibited from speaking Spanish in schools (Anzaldúa, 1990; Crawford, 1991, 2008; Cummins, 2000; Macedo et al., 2003). The colonial legacy continues to affect marginalized groups linguistically and culturally, especially with the rise of the English-only movement (Macedo et al., 2003). According to Macedo and colleagues (2003), in the United States, languages other than the hegemonic English language have been attacked by white conservative intellectuals, such as E. D. Hirsch Jr. (1987), who have fiercely rejected multiculturalism and bilingualism and advocated for a "common culture" (Hirsch, 1987). Thus, one must ask, who exactly has been benefiting from the Western form of democracy?

The noble idea of democracy needs to be a reality not only for those who speak the so-called Standard English, who own the means of production and, thus, control the U.S. political apparatus, but also for those whose native languages have been attacked and whose voices have been silenced. As Chomsky (1994, 2007) contends, democracy is a myth when a minority group in powerful positions has accumulated the wealth of a country and has used the corporate media and the police to manipulate and silence the voice of the majority so they will not revolt against social injustice. These practices violate the core values and principles that shape and constitute the spirit of a democratic society. As Eric Williams (1993), the late prime minister of Trinidad and Tobago, points out:

> Democracy means the obligation of the minority to recognize the right of the majority. Democracy means responsibility of the government to its citizens, the protection of the citizens from the exercise of arbitrary power and the violation of human freedoms and individual rights. (p. 266)

Williams' definition of democracy is yet to be meaningful to those who have been linguistically and racially discriminated against and exploited in a capitalist, neoliberal state in which the wealthy, including CEOs of major corporations, have influenced many institutions, such as schools, the workplace, and the political apparatus. These issues are central to the arguments that Noam Chomsky made in a dialogue I had with him. In this dialogue, Chomsky and I explore issues, such as democracy, schooling, and U.S. domestic and foreign policies. To substantiate the points made throughout the chapter about language, schooling, and democracy, it is worth providing some excerpts from this dialogue, which was conducted with Noam Chomsky for a book project aimed at establishing the link between school, democracy, and language, among other things (Orelus, 2011a).

Language, U.S. School System, and Democracy

Orelus: How do you see the link between the U.S. contested form of democracy and schooling?

Reframing the Debate on Democratic, Educational, and Linguistic Rights | 35

Chomsky: Well, for one thing, what's taught in the classroom is that the U.S. is leading democracy and supports democracy everywhere. In fact, that's not just in the classroom; that's also taught in graduate school. And it's just not true. So one way in which it impacts the classroom is just by inculcating doctoral fabrications, but also the structure of schooling tends to be pretty undemocratic. Let's take the No Child Left Behind legislation. That's just training children to be in the Marine Corps, that is, not to be creative and independent people. That's its nature.

Orelus: You are referring to the No Child Left Behind Act, which is basically all about testing. Many teachers feel that they have to teach to the test; otherwise, they might run the danger of losing their jobs. Would you agree with this assertion?

Chomsky: That's right. The teachers are disciplined. They, in turn, have to discipline the students in order to regurgitate materials that they are supposed to memorize. That's not teaching. I mean you just don't do that. In places where there is a real effort to educate like, say, a graduate education and sciences program, you don't do that. Students are supposed to participate; they're supposed to challenge themselves and teachers; they're supposed to inquire. They don't repeat the lectures and tests.

Orelus: I want to change the subject a little bit. I'm going to move from what we've been talking about for the last 20 minutes to language issues. Do you see any link between language and the neoliberal agenda of the U.S. government?

Chomsky: Anything we do involves language. Of course the terminology and the rhetoric are in language. It does reflect the ideology, power, and so on. For example, the last interview I had about an hour ago, it was a long interview on what are the right measures to use in responding and protecting the country from terrorism and combating terrorism. I spent probably the whole interview trying to explain that's just the wrong question. If you want to stop terrorism, stop participating in it. That's the simple way to reduce terrorism. Secondly, if it's the terrorism of others that you're worried about, then find out what the reasons for it are and deal with them. But if you just ask, it's as if the doctors said, "I'm going to inoculate you with poisons. Now how should I treat you after that?" I mean, you have to treat someone after they put poisons in their body, that's not the right question. All that is in language is the word terror, meaning what they do to us, not what we do to them, which is often much worse. And they don't ask about the sources of their terror, they just combat it with force, either domestically or internationally. That's a way of saying we don't care about the problem. And it's the same for everything else like democracy. It's nothing profound. Language is used in ways that reflect the power interests.

Orelus: Where does culture fit in? You were referring to how language has been used to lie and/or oppress people. What role does culture play in that?

Chomsky: Generally, cultural properties, which are largely sustained on the base of power interest, although there are other factors, shape the way people think, the way they respond, the way they react, the way policies are made, and so on. How could it fail to be true? Well, we could say more about it, but there is nothing profound to say about these topics. I mean, intellectuals do produce complicated texts and polysyllabic words and so on, but, basically, what we understand, it's pretty straightforward. It can be said simply, where it's obvious to everyone.

Orelus: Let me ask you a question about the dominant aspect of the English language. As you know, there are some languages that are more valued than others. For example, the U.S. and the British English have been perceived as Standard English, whereas other Englishes spoken in other countries are seen as inferior. So as a linguist, where do you stand on this issue?

Chomsky: First of all, that's true now; it wasn't true a century ago. A century ago, British English was the standard and the American English was just a kind of dialect. Well, what changed? Who was the most powerful country in the world a century ago? Who's the most powerful country in the world today? Then it was Britain, now it's the U.S. Like I said, there's nothing profound about these things. They're on the surface. English is the most dominant language, because the United States is the richest and, by far, the most powerful country in the world. So sure, English is the dominant language. I mean, not Swahili.

Orelus: So clearly there is a link between language and power. So whichever country has more power tends to use its language to dominate others?

Chomsky: Well, that's the way national languages are formed. I saw people in Italy speak kind of what was once a dialect of Florence, not the dozens of other Italian languages that are around. It's because of the presence of state formation and the formation of the dominant culture and so on. I mean, you hear people talk a lot about endangered languages. Languages are dying all over the world, which is a serious problem. They talk mostly about indigenous languages dying, which is true; they are dying off very fast. But the same is true for languages in Europe. I mean, they are dying off very quickly just because of the establishment of a more powerful central state.

In this dialogue, Professor Chomsky critically analyzes the hegemonic aspect of language and illuminates the unequal power relations between dominant and subjugated languages. He also talks about the correlation between language and power. Specifically, Chomsky shows the way and the extent to which languages spoken by the white dominant class in powerful countries, such as the United States, Great Britain, and France, tend to dominate languages perceived and treated as subaltern languages. Finally, Chomsky unveils the antidemocratic nature of the U.S. form of democracy, arguing that it only works for the rich, and that people, especially ordinary people, are only given the illusion that they are living in a democratic society. Drawing on Chomsky's argument, it can be further argued that the U.S. government is very hypocritical in the sense that it has been trying to impose its form of electoral democracy on other countries when, in fact, there is no participatory democracy in the United States (Carr, 2011).

Toward a Democratic and a Linguistically Equitable Society

Drawing on the arguments articulated previously, I ask: Is it ironic that, despite the widespread belief that the United States is a melting pot and a democratic country, certain languages labeled as minority have been under attack and relegated to a "subaltern position" (Spivak, 1988)? Gloria Anzaldúa's (1990) linguistic and xenophobic experience with an Anglo teacher illustrates the persistent attack of minority languages by dominant groups, including teachers, who have embraced the ideology informing the English-only movement. Anzaldúa recounted her struggle with an Anglo teacher who forbade her from speaking Spanish in class. She states:

> I remember being caught speaking Spanish at recess—that was good for three licks on the knuckles with a sharp ruler. I remember being sent to the corner of the classroom for "talking back" to the Anglo teacher when all I was trying to do was tell her how to pronounce my name. "If you want to be American, speak 'American.' If you don't like it, go back to Mexico where you belong." (p. 203)

Anzaldúa's experience with the Anglo teacher clearly illuminates how those who believe in and embrace the English-only movement have committed symbolic linguistic and cultural violence (Bourdieu, 1991) against marginalized groups by trying to silence their voices, prohibiting them from speaking their mother tongues. Moreover, her experience shows that language is not simply about uttering words but is intrinsically linked to ideology, culture, and power relations (Bourdieu, 1990; Darder, 2011; Foucault, 1980; Gramsci, 1971).

Equally important, the linguistic discrimination that Anzaldúa faced and countless others continue to face in school puts into question the belief that the United States is a free and democratic country. In a country that has been called democratic and free, people should not be threatened and punished for speaking their native tongues. Prohibiting a person from speaking his or her language in a "democratic country" suggests that one is free in "the land of the free" as long as he or she does not speak Spanish, Creole, or other subjugated languages and dialects. I argue that prohibiting people from speaking their native languages contradicts the belief that the United States is a democratic country, unless democracy simply means capitalism in the United States.

Unfortunately, although Anzaldúa's experience with her Anglo teacher happened several decades ago, it is still relevant, for minority students continue to experience linguistic discrimination in this so-called democratic country. Attack against minority native languages is not a simple matter, and I concur with Darder (2012), who states:

> Language domination silences student voices and seriously curtails their active participation in school life. With few opportunities to enter into dialogue, to build on their pre-existing home knowledge, or to reflect on their lived experiences, many working-class bicultural students are left marginalized in their classrooms. (p. 37)

What Darder argues speaks, to a great extent, to the problematic and divisive nature of the language issue in my native land, Haiti.

For instance, French, the imposed language of the French colonizer, is valued over Haitian Creole, the native tongue of most Haitians like myself. Because of this colonial legacy, those who speak only Creole (the vast majority of whom tend to be the poor dark-skinned Haitians) are looked down on and have very limited access, if any, to sociopolitical mobility in Haiti. By contrast, the middle and upper class Haitians who have embraced and mastered the French language have historically been those dominating Haiti's economic and political systems (Orelus, 2011b).

Along the same lines, it is worth noting that the French spoken by poor working-class Haitians does not hold the same social-class status as the French spoken by those who belong to the upper middle class and upper class, especially those who have been privileged enough to study abroad in French-speaking countries, such as France and Belgium (Orelus, 2011b). To further complicate the language issue in Haiti, it is equally important to mention that some level of linguistic discrimination based on accents sometimes happens among poor urban and rural working-class Haitians. Depending on the regions they are from, their French or Creole accent may be different. Those who believe they speak French or French Creole with the "right accent," meaning close to the Parisian accent, sometimes assume they are linguistically superior to, or more sophisticated than, those who do not (Orelus, 2011b). I use these examples to show that, like in the United States and elsewhere, there is a serious language and class divide in Haiti.

Conclusion

In closing, I contend that democracy, particularly a participatory form of democracy, is worth fighting for so people can live in a society in which their languages, cultures, and "funds of knowledge" (Moll, 1988) are respected and incorporated in the school curriculum; in which workers, particularly workers of color, are not brutally exploited; and, more importantly, in which ordinary citizens are part of the political decision-making processes affecting their lives rather than being passive spectators of these processes. Unless these *sine qua non* conditions are fully met, the concept of democracy will merely remain an illusion created by those in power who, historically, have used empty rhetoric to gain the consent of, and given false hope to, the masses to maintain the status quo (Gramsci, 1971; Marx, 1994). Building on the arguments made in this chapter, Chapter 4 talks in depth about the experience of learning and teaching in a colonial-based, capitalist test-driven school system.

4

Decolonizing Schools and Our Mentality: Counter Narratives from a Colonized Subject

There was often not the slightest relationship between the child's written world, which was also the language of his schooling, and the world of his immediate environment in the family and the community. For a colonial child, the harmony existing between these three aspects of language as communication was irrevocably broken. This resulted in the disassociation of the sensibility of that child from his natural and social environment, what we might call colonial alienation. The alienation became reinforced in the teaching of history, geography, music, where bourgeois Europe was always the centre of the universe (wa Thiong'o, 1986, p. 7).

If the inequities of colonial rule have not been erased, it is perhaps premature to proclaim the demise of colonialism. A country may be both postcolonial (in the sense of being formally independent) and neo-colonial (in the sense of remaining economically and/or culturally dependent) at the same time. We cannot dismiss the importance of either formal decolonization, or the fact that unequal relations of colonial rule are reinscribed in the contemporary imbalances between "first" and "third" world nations. The new global order does not depend upon direct rule. However, it does allow the economic, cultural, and (to varying degrees) political penetration of some countries by others. This makes it debatable whether once-colonized countries can be seen as properly "postcolonial." (Loomba, 2002, p. 7)

> Neocolonialism denotes a continuing economic hegemony that means that the postcolonial state remains in a situation of dependence on its former masters, and that the former masters continue to act in a colonialist manner towards formerly colonized states. Was there merely a change in form rather than substance? Decolonization in this analysis would really only correspond to the shift between what Gramsci called political and civil societies, that is from a society controlled by military force to one that no longer required such physical force because the hegemony of the ruling class was sufficiently established at a cultural, ideological, economic and political level for it to operate by means of prestige and active consent. (Young, 2006, p. 45)

> Neocolonialism is . . . the worst form of imperialism. For those who practise it, it means power without responsibility and for those who suffer from it, it means exploitation without redress. (Nkrumah, 1965, p. 11)

For many critical educators, colonialism is still at work; its legacy continues to shape the practices of many institutions, such as schools, governments, churches, workplaces, and the mass media (Fanon, 1965; Kempf & Dei, 2006; wa Thiong'o, 1986). Colonialism has been implemented through different educational, socio-economic, and political policies that have had a negative impact on the school systems of many countries, particularly formerly colonized countries as well as those that are currently occupied (Dei, 2009; Loomba, 2002; Nkrumah, 1965; Orelus, 2007). The educational, socio-economic, political, and cultural disaster that colonialism has engendered may not be as obvious as neoliberalism, for example, partly because those in power have used the corporate media to gain the consent of the people, including the poor, leading them to believe they have benefited from global capitalism and the "free market."

However, those who have presence of mind and are, thus, able to critically reflect on their direct experience with neocolonialism know this system mostly works for those who have created it (Fanon, 1963, 1965; Loomba, 2002; wa Thiong'o, 1986; Young, 2006). In light of this, I draw on personal and professional experiences teaching and being educated in a colonial-based, capitalist test-driven school system to examine the ways in which and the degree to which the legacy of colonialism continues to impact the learning, the subjectivity, and cultural and material conditions of colonial subjects, including linguistically and culturally diverse students. I critically reflect on and examine my mis-education in a colonial-based school system. I go further to articulate what a democratic and participatory form of education should look like in a classroom context, arguing that this form of education aims at preparing students to become well-educated and informed critical citizens.

My Mis-Education in a Colonial-Based School System: A Critical Autoethnographical Reflection

As a high school student who was educated in a school system that mimicked and followed the rules and teaching codes of the French colonial model of education, I was taught to believe that knowledge is something transferred mechanically from teachers to pupils. I was not allowed to challenge and engage in a dialogue with my teachers and peers during class. Instead, I was expected to sit, listen, and copy what the teachers wrote on the board. I was also expected to memorize and regurgitate what I "learned." Needless to say, the teaching procedure involved rote behavior, and most of my teachers failed to create space in which I could use what I "learned" and link it to real life situations beyond the classroom walls and the collapsing fences that encircled the school building. I was not encouraged to make decisions on my own, to be a creative and an independent thinker, or to be a problem solver. Although there was ample room in my classrooms for plenty of meaningless activities, there was little room for teacher-student and student-student interactions.

As an example, I had to follow whatever my teachers assigned to me. My work was evaluated based on how well I followed what teachers did in class. I was mostly tested on what I copied in my notebooks, even though my teacher's explanation was often unclear. I felt that the poor thinking, writing, and reading skills I acquired could only prepare me for routine and menial types of jobs in the real world. Freire (1993), in *Pedagogy of the Oppressed*, eloquently synthesizes this oppressive style of education. Freire summarizes:

> the teacher teaches and the students are taught;
> the teacher knows everything and the students know nothing;
> the teacher thinks and the students are taught about;
> the teacher talks and the students listen—meekly;
> the teacher disciplines and the students are disciplined;
> the teacher chooses and enforces his choice, and the students comply;
> the teacher acts and the students have the illusion of acting through the action of the teacher;
> the teacher chooses the program content, and the students (who are not consulted) adapt to it;
> the teacher confuses the authority of knowledge with his or her own professional authority, which she or he sets in opposition to the freedom of the students;

the teacher is the Subject of the learning process, while the pupils are mere objects. (p. 54)

Similarly, in *Cries from the Corridor*, McLaren (1980) describes the horrible and anti-democratic conditions in which poor urban school students are expected to learn. McLaren argues these students often have to memorize and regurgitate what they "learn" via rote teaching and learning mechanisms. Those who manage to do so are usually considered the best students. At some point during my high school and college years, I was perceived as one of these students, for I managed to regurgitate what I was taught. It was not until I came across and avidly read *Emile ou de L'education*, by French writer Jean-Jacques Rousseau, that I realized I was being mis-educated. Specifically, thanks to this book, I was finally able conclude that the form of education that I was receiving from my teachers was essentially domesticating my mind. The overarching argument Rousseau (1966) makes in *Emile ou de L'education* is that pupils should be allowed to learn at their own pace and should not be expected to engage in any learning endeavor that is abstract and meaningless to their lives. Education, in this sense, is conceived as a self-discovery learning process in which pupils explore their learning without any forcible control by a teacher. Kneller (1964) captures Rousseau's philosophy of education, stating:

> [Rousseau] stated that it was useless to expect a child to indulge abstract intellectual pursuits until he had reached the age of reason. Instead, a child should learn the things that he is capable of understanding through personal discovery. Followers of Rousseau urged teachers to connect what the child learned in school with what he would experience at home in his community, that is, to connect education and life. (pp. 104–105)

Although, later in my learning curve, I partially rejected Rousseau's view on education, at that time, I found his radical philosophy of education refreshing and inspiring, especially after being mis-educated by almost all my high school and college teachers. I later refuted some of Rousseau's view on education, because I felt and still feel it is essentially a laissez-faire learning style that he consciously or unconsciously promoted through his book, which is worth reading nonetheless. Unlike Rousseau, I believe that, if students are to learn, they need to be clearly guided and challenged by their teachers, although there are people who manage to learn on their own. However, even the so-called autodidacts do not construct knowledge alone. They do so collectively with others, whether in school settings or other settings.

Furthermore, before I became familiar with the scholarly works of the Russian philosopher Bakhtin (1986), the American educator John Dewey (1997), and the

Brazilian educator Paulo Freire (1993), who believe in co-construction of knowledge, my learning experience had already taught me that knowledge is constructed collectively. In other words, I already knew, before being introduced to the work of these theorists, that knowledge is not something automatically passed on from a teacher, who is believed to know everything, to a student, who does not know much or, worse yet, does not know anything.

In *The Republic* Plato showed that knowledge is dialectically constructed through dialogue between teachers and students and/or mentors and mentees. Specifically, Plato (2008) demonstrated that, through open dialogue, a mentee learns from his/her mentor and vice versa. The dialogue in which Plato and Socrates engaged is a case in point. By creating space for a genuine dialogue between himself (Socrates) and his mentee (Plato), Socrates does not merely guide, teach, and challenge Plato, but he also learns from Plato. Although a person might think that Socrates is playing the role of a master by dialoguing with Plato, Socrates also learns from Plato in the process. In my view, teachers' philosophies of education and teaching practices should reflect the dialogical learning relationship that Socrates and Plato established as teacher and pupil. In other words, as Kneller (1964) argues:

> The Socratic method is the ideal mode of education, since by it the student learns what he personally asserts to be true. The teacher-pupil relationship becomes intimate and personal. The teacher persuades the student to think by questioning him about his beliefs, by setting before him other beliefs and thus forcing him to probe the workings of his own mind. In this way the student accepts the truth, but only because it is true for him. (p. 70)

My Evolving Philosophy of Education and Teaching

My philosophy of education is grand yet simple. I believe that teachers first and foremost should be aware of what they are teaching students to become. In other words, before engaging in the act of teaching, they need to ask themselves questions, such as:

- Am I going to teach my students a set of fragmented knowledge and how to regurgitate it to people as tangible evidence that they are "smart" and prepared to meet certain academic, intellectual, and professional expectations, and fit certain social norms?

- Am I going to help them develop critical thinking skills to dismantle this set of fragmented knowledge and reconstruct it based on their prior knowledge, lived experience, imagination, and own understanding of it?
- Am I going to encourage my students to take intelligent risks informed by their intellectual curiosity and personal interests?
- Am I going to censure their learning by expecting them to open up their minds and fill them up with a pre-packaged information and knowledge that I prepare for and impose on them?
- Am I going to encourage them to interrogate that information and knowledge to figure out what piece they can relate to their interests and goals?
- Am I going to single them out in my class for daring to question what I teach them and for disagreeing with my teaching approach and philosophy of education?
- More importantly, am I going to be willing to engage in a dialogue with them to find out more about their previous learning experience, different approaches of teaching and philosophy of education, and be open to learn from them new ideas about learning and teaching?
- Am I going to be continuously stuck in my comfort teaching zone, expecting my students to passively receive and repeat, like parrots, the knowledge I pass on to them?
- Am I going to cultivate intellectual and moral courage, respect for human intelligence, and self-awareness so I am prepared to treat my students as intellectual beings who have the innate ability to think critically, reflect actively, and decide for themselves with whom I can deconstruct knowledge, while constructing new one in the process?

Teachers guided by a progressive philosophy of education help students develop creative and critical thinking skills to continuously question their own learning, which should always be in the making. These teachers assume a responsible task to help students understand that education is not about how many theories they "learn" through rote memorization. Rather, it is about challenging students to interrogate, constantly search, and figure out how these theories come into being; how the students can connect them to their interests, intellectual needs, and life; and how the students can use these theories to effect social change. Teachers who teach students to become critical and independent thinkers also take on a gigantic teaching task to help students develop sociopolitical, cultural, and historical awareness and consciousness to challenge social norms instead of preparing them to become mere docile adapters to these norms. Equally crucial, progressive educators are those who urge students to discover their own paths through continuous search and exploration of novel ideas while providing genuine support and mentorship.

What students are expected to learn in school is meaningless to the extent they are not able to read their own meaning into it—linking their own experience and interests to it. Students study and learn best when the relevance of what they study or are expected to learn is made clear to them or, better yet, when they themselves see its relevance to their intellectual interests, needs, or curiosity. Stated otherwise, something is meaningful to students so long as they feel they can connect it to their own real-life situations and those of others.

Since real life situations might change as they go through higher stages in their academic and intellectual journey, students should be encouraged and helped by their teachers to cultivate intellectual flexibility and openness to try novel ideas, deconstruct prior ideas, construct new ideas, and take on new challenges. Teachers should help develop intellectual awareness so students understand that the knowledge they acquire, as a result of personal, intellectual search and interaction with teachers and peers, is not a fixed entity. Simply stated, students need to fully comprehend that knowledge is not like a beautiful piece of art purchased at an art studio, taken home, hung on the wall, and left there. Rather, knowledge is acquired through social, cultural, and historical transactions with people and exposure to varying sources of literature. Although knowledge should be highly appreciated and valued, it needs to be continuously expanded on, re-examined, questioned, and constantly tested.

As noted, students should not be expected to develop all of these critical skills on their own. They should receive assistance and guidance from teachers. However, for all this to be a reality, educators need to make a conscious effort to reach out to and know their students, which is only possible through genuine dialogical relationships. Knowing their students enables educators to have a sound understanding of their learning styles; their cultural, linguistic, and historical repertoires; and their prior knowledge; as well as how to help them build on that knowledge. Building on students' various repertoires and prior knowledge facilitates the learning process of students and the teaching practices of teachers and, most importantly, validates students' identities while strengthening their confidence and self-esteem.

Equally important, teachers have a professional and moral obligation to find ways to make the school curriculum accessible and meaningful to students whose backgrounds might not match the content of this curriculum. In other words, since education is the essence of life but not the means and the end to it, for students to relate what they learn in school to their lived experience, school materials should be based on real life circumstances, not on abstract ideas. To this end, it is critically important that students and teachers collectively question how school materials and curriculum are selected and developed—what shapes them and where they come from. It is equally imperative that teachers interrogate which voices are represented in these written curricula, as occupied and colonized students' voices often are not represented in the learning materials required in classes.

Since "the curriculum is often seen as the driving force for instructional practice, the framework within which day-to-day decisions are made" (Auerbach, 1995, p. 15), should school materials, such as textbooks and school curricula, then emerge from the students' world and lived experience? In other words, should school curricula be student centered to allow space for students' active participation and interaction with other students and teachers? As Auerbach (1995) maintains, when teachers "start from the students to the curriculum rather from the curriculum to the students," (p. 16) students are able to construct their own knowledge and act on it.

Drawing on Auerbach's contention, I argue that to understand what fundamentally causes the mis-education of students, it is educationally vital that a person looks closely at what is going on in the classroom in terms of how teachers teach, interact with, and construct or fail to construct knowledge with students. I am not implying that the mis-education of students should be placed on teachers' shoulders alone, because such an argument takes responsibilities off the school system, policy makers, and the government, overlooking other factors, such as the negative effects of the legacy of Western colonialism and neoliberal education policies have had on the learning of students, particularly linguistically and culturally diverse students, and teaching practices of teachers, especially urban school teachers. However, teachers' teaching practices, attitude towards students, level of trust in students, and level of investment in the learning of each student needed to be taken into consideration, for these factors play a crucial role in students' academic achievement.

Lessons Learned

As a social justice educator, it took me a long time before I finally understood the vital role a culturally relevant and meaningful curriculum plays in student learning. It also took me a long time to understand how crucial it is to know, first and foremost, my students and use their prior knowledge as a building block to help them achieve academically. I came to that understanding through my personal schooling experience; the contact with the great works of Dewey (1997), Vygotsky (1978), and Freire (1993); the acquisition of various teaching methods and theories in multicultural education articulated by Nieto and Bode (2011), Grant and Sleeter, (2007), and Sleeter (2005); and through constant self-questioning on what kind of teacher I wanted to become and how I would teach my students to become what they want to be.

Before I became a teacher, I questioned whether I had the human understanding and political and cultural awareness to teach effectively. I also wondered if I had a strong enough sense of social justice, responsibility, and commitment to begin this long journey. This was when the immensity of the teaching profession seemed really challenging to me, for I knew whatever I taught my students in the classroom would impact their lives. These puzzling questions were left unanswered, until I started teaching culturally and linguistically diverse students from poor working class backgrounds. Working with these students made me realize that I could not teach them these subjects without considering their cultural background and identity, which constitute an integral part of their learning process.

My Experience Teaching Linguistically and Culturally Diverse Students

I taught minority students in the most marginalized high school in Boston, Massachusetts. This experience helped me better understand how racial and social inequality impacts the learning and academic growth of poor minority students and poor white students. This high school was underfunded; so many caring and dedicated teachers had to teach their poor students of color and whites under horrible working conditions. For example, school materials were scarce; consequently many of my colleagues and I had to use our own money to buy school supplies. Worse, many of us were forced to leave our teaching jobs because of budget cuts. I was one of the teachers laid off. I question why schools in poor neighborhood serving poor children of color and poor whites are always the first to drastically suffer from state and federal budget cuts. Should these schools not be the least affected by these cuts?

I was fortunate to be hired as a bilingual reading and ESL teacher at a high school located in Boston, Massachusetts. This experience has shaped my teaching experience and philosophy. I remember the intensity of inner fear I experienced when I first became a high school teacher, especially during my first year. Although my master's degree provided the necessary critical and analytical tools to look at the world with a critical eye, I did not feel it prepared me to teach. Consequently, during my first year as a teacher, I experienced fear that nearly paralyzed me. I incessantly questioned if it was ethical to dare to teach students, especially marginalized groups of students, as I did not feel adequately prepared to do so. Suddenly, this type of self-questioning led me to reflect on many ill-prepared teachers I had in high school and even in college. I did not learn much from them. Hence, I did not want to reproduce what I was done to me—mis-educated by poorly prepared teachers.

However, I was and am still sure that I have much love and passion for teaching and, more importantly, for co-constructing knowledge with students. Such passion and love enabled me as a first-year teacher to make the effort to find enough humility in myself to reach out to colleagues, especially those who had extensive teaching experience. Some of these colleagues helped me tremendously by sharing teaching material resources, whereas others served as my mentors.

For example, during my first and second years as a high school teacher, I asked two of my colleagues, who were like mentors to me, if I could come to their classrooms and observe how they taught. They both happily honored my request. They also came to observe my class and gave constructive feedback on my teaching methods. In fact, one invited me to come to his class during recess so he could share some of his teaching methods and strategies, which I experimented with in my reading and ESL classes. These colleagues were very kind, friendly, and welcoming and showed genuine concern for their students, who were from poor working class backgrounds, living in marginalized neighborhoods. However, I was soon disappointed by one, who made a value judgment about one of his students. He said that this student, who apparently was not doing well in his class due to a temporary language barrier and culture shock, should drop out of high school and go learn how to be a mechanic, because he did not think this student was college material, suggesting he had very low expectations for this student.

As a teacher, I felt hurt. It was sad to hear such a harmful comment from a colleague for whom I had much respect and to whom I was and am still grateful for his mentorship. At first, I wondered whether I should distance myself because of his insensitive comment, which is, in my view, a deficit view of his student. Because my colleague was white and middle class and this student was black from a poor working class background, the idea of this teacher possibly being racist and classist inevitably crossed my mind. I challenged such a thought, however, asking myself, "Could a teacher like my colleague, who said he cared for his students, be racist and classist?" I am still puzzled by this question, to which I have not yet found an answer.

Reflecting on the example of my former high school colleague, I feel that, by remaining silent, I was in complicity with my colleague's dehumanizing way of looking at his student's potential. I regret not having taken a stand for this student by challenging my colleague's comment. In my mind, by not challenging him, I thought I was being tolerant and respectful to him as a dear colleague and a mentor.

Now, reflecting back on this professional experience as an educator, I have come to the conclusion that teachers who are biased and lack political and cultural awareness can negatively affect students' self-worth and the course of their learning. In other words, a teacher can psychologically and educationally break his or her students into small pieces, especially those working in schools that are colonial-based and corporate driven. Echoing Freire, I argue that my colleague's comment about his student suggests he did not have a humanizing approach to education.

The majority of the students who attended this high school were African Americans and Cape Verdeans from poor working-class backgrounds. During my 3 years teaching at the high school, teachers were pressured to teach to the test. Students, particularly my bilingual students, were taking tests almost every 2 months, regardless of their limited English skills. I was required to use a scripted curriculum to teach my students how to read. The curriculum required giving students a pre-test on Mondays and a post-test on Fridays. These tests were designed to help my students build their vocabulary. This curriculum, however, did not allow me space to engage my students in sufficient critical literacy activity. Despite my opposition to these tests, I had to administer them to my bilingual students, including those who just arrived in the United States and could barely read, write, and speak English. In fact, in my class, there were many students who did not receive formal education in their first language. For this category of students, taking these tests was much more painful.

When I was not under the surveillance of my supervisor and the school's assistant principals, who came to my class whenever they wished, I engaged my students in activities I thought would be meaningful to their lives. For example, I knew that what I taught had to matter to them; therefore, I incorporated thoughts and ideas generated from their classroom group discussions into my lesson plans. Writing exercises and class discussions were usually generated from the questions I encouraged them to discuss about their family, living conditions at home and in their neighborhood, and the socio-economic and political realities they faced in their daily lives. The concerns they expressed and the questions they asked in class about these factors were part of the classroom experience. For example, my students were always eager to talk about their culture and experience as immigrants. Thus, to make what I taught in the classroom meaningful, I produced a unit about culture and immigration. They wrote short essays in which they compared their culture with American culture and talked about their experience as immigrants living in the United States. I was often amazed to see that all of my students were actively engaged in the class discussion and activities.

As a result, I learned that teachers have an obligation to find ways to teach their students what is practical and relevant to their lives. From this experience, I have concluded that it is crucial that the school system has well-trained educators capable of effectively teaching students necessary writing, reading, and critical thinking skills so these students are prepared to face multiple challenges in the real world. Teaching students with various ethnic, cultural, linguistic, and social class backgrounds has made me fully aware that students need full support and encouragement to preserve their cultural heritage and identity. This might help them connect with the past, make sense of the present, and prepare for the future.

Conclusion

I hope that these narratives about my learning and teaching experiences in a neocolonial, capitalist, test-driven school system will not discourage the reader from believing that educators, especially those who believe in social justice, can play the role of agents of social change by helping students develop a language of hope to believe that the creation of a better school system and society is possible. I also hope these narratives do not dissuade the reader that there are educators who have helped students develop a language of critique, enabling many to counter the negative effects of the colonial legacy on their learning. Although the neocolonial context of countries whose school systems continue to be affected by the colonial legacy entrenched in the capitalist system still exists, many progressive teachers have risked their jobs to ensure that we have a democratic school system in which students are treated fairly and are given the opportunities to fulfill their potential irrespective of their backgrounds. This is what has given hope to many teachers, parents, and students. We need to build on this hope for a better future in which all students have the opportunity to attend well-resourced schools and receive a high-quality education, regardless of gender; cultural, linguistic, social class, and racial background.

5

Beyond Linguoracism and White Hegemony: Affirming Multiple Identities and Languages

Linguoracism in discursive practices is realized partly by representing cultural inheritance as resembling biological inheritance. Cultural systems, including language, are associated with racial collectives, as commonly expressed in utterances such as "Greek is the language of the Hellenic race." Yet, the literature devoted to the investigation of racist practices often excludes language in its agenda. While recognizing that language viewed as discourse is the basic means through which racism is shaped and maintained, discussions of the elusive term "race" do not explicitly include language as a distinguishing feature of its social construction. Indeed, in some cases, it is not. (Macedo et al., 2003, p. 91)

Values are the basis of a people's identity, their sense of particularity as members of the human race. All this is carried by language. Language as culture is the collective memory bank of a people's experience in history. Culture is almost indistinguishable from the language that makes possible its genesis, growth, banking, articulation, and indeed its transmission from one generation to the next. (wa Thiong'o, 1986, p. 15)

"Dirty nigger!" Or simply, "Look, a Negro." I came into the world imbued with the will to find a meaning in things, my spirit filled with desire to attain to the source of the world, and then I found that I was an object in the midst of other objects. (Fanon, 1967, p. 109)

So, if you really want to hurt me, talk bad about my language. Ethnic identity is twin skin to linguistic identity—I am my language. Until I can take pride in my language, I cannot take pride in myself. (Anzaldúa, 2007, p. 18)

I know it is not the English language that hurts me, but what the oppressors do with it, how they shape it to become a territory that limits and defines, how they make it a weapon that can shame, humiliate, and colonize. (hooks, 1994, p. 168)

Some of those who migrated to the west, or their children, subsequently attended educational institutions with a still active sense of coming from what were then regarded as the cultural and political margins and peripheries. They did not respond by accepting the status quo and assimilating seamlessly into the culture in which they now found themselves: rather, armed with the aura of the activism and self-empowerment of the national liberation movements, they began to ask awkward questions about western history and the implicit assumptions of western knowledges and to articulate their ontological engagement with tricontinental knowledge with forms of resistance to the racism and disempowerment that are part of the daily life on any immigrant. (Young, 2006, p. 62)

Some have argued that identity is the reflection of a person's sense of self. This chapter expands on that premise, examining it from a racially, linguistically, socially, culturally, and cross-border perspective (Ahmed, 2000; Anzaldúa, 2007; Hamzeh, 2012). A person's identity necessarily encompasses his or her racial, social, historical, sexual, and cultural characteristics and growth (Hamzeh, 2012; Appiah, 2005; Castells, 2006; Holland, Lachicotte, Skinner & Cain, 2003; Norton, 2000). Understood as such, identity is not static; it is fluid and dialectical. Furthermore, identity is contextual, connected to time. Hence, as a person's social, cultural, or political milieu changes, identity evolves in tandem.

This is irrefutably true in the experience of many immigrants of color, including myself. For example, since I immigrated to the United States in the mid-1990s, my identity has evolved tremendously. Specifically, it has profoundly shifted from being Haitian to being black, a foreigner, and "an alien"—identifying constructs that persist even as I have become a U.S. citizen and university professor at an institution at which I often feel like a "minority within minorities" (Montero-Sieburth, 2000, p. 228). That is, although several of my colleagues in my department are labeled "minority" because of their racial, linguistic, gender, and ethnic backgrounds and sexual orientation, I am the only black professor with a recognizably foreign accent.

By saying I often feel like a "minority within minorities," I neither intend to fall into self-pity, nor am I seeking compassion, empathy, or sympathy. It is not my goal to merely represent myself as "oppressed" (Freire, 1993) or as a victim of a system that often silences the voice of "the subaltern" (Spivak, 1988) and lacks space in which they can affirm their multiple identities. The reason I refuse to represent myself merely as a victim is that, although I have experienced racism, linguicism, and xenophobia because of my racial background, native tongue, and country of origin, I am also fully cognizant of both earned and unearned privileges to which I have had access as a heterosexual black male university professor.

Drawing both on my personal narrative as a form of inquiry (Richardson, 2000) and on critical race theory (Bell, 1992, 2009; Delgado, 1989; Delgado & Stefancic, 1995; Gillborn, 2005, 2008; Ladson-Billings, 2004; Leonardo, 2009; Stovall, 2006), I interrogate and critically examine how certain labels have been racially, socially, culturally, and historically constructed and imposed on People of Color, including myself. As feminist and postcolonial scholars, such as bell hooks (1984, 1989), Linda Tuhiwai Smith (1999), Gloria Anzaldúa (2007), Edward Said (1978, 1996, 2000), Chandra Talpade Mohanty (2003), Rodolfo Acuña (2008, 2010), and Alturo Aldama (2001) have eloquently pointed out, the imposition of these labels often leads to people's marginalized position in society. Because various labels have been placed on me, for example, I am often perceived and treated as the "other," and my voice has consequently been silenced at times.

Professors and colleagues at institutions at which I studied and have taught have often performed and behaved as if they have access to power and knowledge (Foucault, 1995), and many have attempted to use their senior status to oppress me by silencing my voice. It is, therefore, imperative that I intervene to counter this form of oppression and tell my resistant stories, because, as Coloma (2008) argues, "The desire to speak for oneself is especially important for marginalized individuals and communities that have been imagined and represented by those who occupy dominant positions of power" (p. 11). Coloma adds, "For the marginalized, at stake is the right of self-definition and self-determination. The refusal to be silent is a necessary and vigilant act of affirmation and resistance" (p.12). Building on Coloma's views, I argue that the liberation of marginalized groups from racial, linguistic, and class oppression cannot be achieved while remaining silent, whether because of self-censorship or pressure from by those in power. Therefore, exploring the possibility of articulating their own story is a great step toward self-liberation.

Targeted: Toward the Dis-Alienation of Racial and Linguistic Identities

Many immigrants of color have faced two major challenges: being black or brown immigrants from third world countries and speaking languages other than the dominant language of their adopted country or speaking the dominant language with a "foreign" accent (Rumbaut & Portes, 2001; Valdés, 2001). I have personally coped with the painful experiences resulting from these racial and linguistic markers. In Haiti, I was merely Haitian and treated as such. However, after I moved to the United States, my identity changed dramatically: I am also black, an immigrant, a minority, and a "boat person," as Haitian immigrants are so often portrayed in the mainstream media. These are social identities, or labels, I did not construct myself. They have been arbitrarily imposed on me, and I have to deal with their repercussions.

I was never referred to as black or, worse, called "nigger" while living in my native land. Therefore, I never had to worry about my blackness or bear the psychological wounds and pain that come along with it (Matsuda, Lawrence, Delgado, & Crenshaw, 1993). However, for the past decade or more that I have been living in the United States, I have been treated primarily as black, regardless of my nationality. I have been socially compelled to constantly worry about my blackness. My black skin has made me a target. By virtue of being black, I have been discriminated against at school and in other settings. I have also been discriminated against because of my nonstandard way of speaking English. Depending on the context, I have been made invisible or visible.

I felt visible when, for example, on my way back home from school on a Thursday afternoon in 1994, a white police officer followed me, pulled me over, handcuffed me, put me in his car, took me to a police station, and detained me for no apparent reason. When I asked the police officer why he pulled me over, he could not give me a clear explanation. Instead, he asked why my eyes were so red. I then replied to him saying, "It has been a long day for me, officer, at school, and I am exhausted. This is why my eyes are red." He dismissed what I told him by saying, "I have been busy all day too, and my eyes are not red." I remained quiet for a while and then protested by shouting, "Are you arresting me because I am black?" He pretended that he did not hear what I said, and asked, "What did you say? Anything you say can be used against you."

I was frightened by his reaction, so I remained quiet until we reached the police station at which I was detained for about 6 hours, with no clear explanation given as to why I was taken into custody. While I was waiting for my older brother, who

I called to come and bail me out, the police officer searched my wallet, which he completely emptied. Apparently, because I was not yet proficient in the English language—having been in the United States for a relatively short period of time—the police officer suspected that perhaps I was an undocumented immigrant. I overheard him calling Immigration and Naturalization Services (INS; now called Homeland Security) to check my legal status. Fortunately, the officer could not succeed with his xenophobic plan to spy on me and have me deported, for I had legal documents that allowed me to live here.

When my brother came to the police station inquiring why I was stopped, arrested, and detained, the police officer stated that I was speeding. My brother replied, "Why did not you just give him a ticket? Why is he here?" The police officer responded that I did not stop quickly on time when pulled over and that I stopped on the wrong side of the road, which he stated posed a danger to the lives of other drivers and passengers. I did stop on what he called the wrong side of the road, because I felt compelled to pull over immediately, but I do not recall not stopping on time when he pulled me over.

What the police failed to tell my brother was that, when he pulled me over, I stayed calm in my car, but that he still called for backups and did not ask me why it took me too long to stop. Instead, he asked me why the driver's door of my car was damaged and if the car was mine, even though he already had my driver's license and the car registration in his hands. Finally, the police officer did not tell my brother that he pressured me to tell him why my eyes were red and that he forcibly pulled me out of the car, forced my head against his car, and handcuffed me. My brother left the police station extremely upset, and I was still awfully frightened, trying to wrap my head around the reason(s) the police officer treated me the way he did. I soon realized that my black skin was the visible marker, which led to my unfair arrest and detention.

In *Black Skin, White Masks*, Frantz Fanon (1967) recounted a similar experience he had in France with a white boy and his mother while walking in the street. The white boy, who seemed scared of Fanon's blackness, fearfully called his mother while pointing to Fanon, saying, "Look at the nigger! . . . Mama, a Negro! . . . Hell, he's getting mad. . . . Take no notice, sir, he does not know that you are as civilized as we . . ." (p. 113). Fanon analyzed this racial discrimination he experienced:

> My body was given back to me sprawled out, distorted, recolored, clad in mourning in that white winter day. The Negro is an animal, the Negro is bad, the Negro is mean, the Negro is ugly; look, a nigger, it's cold, the nigger is shivering, the nigger is shivering because he is cold, the little boy is trembling because he is afraid

of the nigger, the nigger is shivering with cold, that cold that goes through your bones, the handsome little boy is trembling because he thinks that the nigger is quivering with rage, the little white boy throws himself into his mother's arms: Mama, the nigger's going to eat me up. (pp. 113–114)

As Fanon's experience with the white boy and his mother illustrates, a person's dark or black skin often makes him or her a target. Moreover, depending on the context, a person's skin tone might make him or her visible or invisible. For instance, while walking in the street in France, Fanon's skin tone made him become visible in the white little boy's eyes. Similarly, in Belchertown, Massachusetts, where I lived for about 1 year, I witnessed the nervousness and fear in my white neighbors' faces each time I opened the main entrance door to the building in which I lived.

Facing Linguistic and Racial Discrimination Courageously

I did not speak English prior to moving to the United States. This is the reality of many people. I vividly remember the challenges I faced learning a new language and adjusting to a new culture. It helped tremendously that I already spoke two languages before immigrating to the United States, for I was able to transfer the knowledge acquired in my native tongue, Haitian Creole, and my first academic language, French, to my target language, English. However, these linguistic assets did not save me from the culture shock I encountered in the United States; nor did they protect me from the xenophobia or linguistic and racial discrimination I experienced in college. I am reminded of a horrible experience I had while presenting a paper in one of my undergraduate classes.

With my limited English-speaking skills, I was required to present my final paper to my monolingual classmates and the instructor. After I finished presenting the paper, the instructor asked my classmates if they had any questions. Several students asked me questions, to which I responded. Then, a white female student, Jennifer, who was sitting next to me, shouted, "I didn't understand anything he was saying; how can I then ask him any questions?" There was a silence that followed. The instructor, who pretended that nothing happened, proceeded to ask if anyone else had any questions for me.

I stood frozen and felt ashamed in front of the whole class after Jennifer made this insensitive comment. What I found particularly shocking about her comment was the fact that no one else seemed to have a problem understanding me, except for her. Furthermore, I was suspicious of Jennifer's comment, because, since the beginning of the semester, she showed a lack of tolerance and respect toward me when I spoke in class. For example, she interrupted me several times as if the questions I was asking or comments I was making were not important or annoyed her.

I went home that day thinking about dropping the class. I even thought about dropping out of college, fearing I would not complete my associate degree at the community college because of my temporary English-language barrier. When I returned to class the following week, I was hoping Jennifer would apologize for humiliating me in front of the class, but she never did. For the remainder of that semester, I became tongue tied and remained silent. I stopped talking in class, fearing my classmates, especially Jennifer, would look down on me for not speaking like they did.

This painful experience has caused my linguistic inferiority complex in the English language. That is, even though I am now fluent and proficient in English, I still question my oral competency and ability in English. I still experience some level of inner fear when I speak English, especially in front of people I barely know. I feel this inner fear even more strongly when speaking with a native speaker when he or she says, "What did you say?" or "Can you repeat what you said, because I didn't understand." Or, it is worse when people say, "You're a professor, really? In what language do you teach? Is it in French?" I have gotten this xenophobic reaction even from people whose second or third language is English and whose accent is much heavier than mine.

It seems to me that uninformed people tend to equate having a "foreign" accent with a lack of intelligence. In other words, if a person does not speak like an "American," that is, like a middle-class, white American, then the person's intelligence has to be questioned and the person's native language, if not English, cannot be appreciated and respected. In my view, this type of attitude has helped the proponents of the English-only movement to attack and eliminate bilingual programs in states such as California, Arizona, and Massachusetts. This attitude has also helped create a stronger climate of xenophobia in the United States.

While I was finishing my associate degree at that community college, I had another painful experience with an English professor, Professor Mathis. I took an English composition class with him after my sister-in-law assured me I would do well in his class. She trusted I would do well based on the fact that I helped my older brother with his English assignments when he was taking the same class with a different professor. Although I was not orally proficient in the English language, I was able to read and write in English fairly well. Furthermore, having already acquired academic discourse in my second language, French, I was able to write in an academic fashion in English, although with some difficulties.

However, despite my strong academic background prior to joining Professor Mathis's class, I had an awful experience taking this English composition class with him. He scorned me numerous times for not speaking English well. He questioned whether I completed my own assignments for his class. He questioned my intelligence. Apparently, he equated my lack of fluency in the English language to lower intelligence. Although he encouraged my classmates to meet with him during his office hours, he did not offer me the same.

I could not stop thinking that Professor Mathis was xenophobic and racist and that he did not want to waste his time meeting with someone who did not look and speak like him. In his class, I was the only black person and the only student for whom English was not my first language. Determined to not give up and drop his class, I took initiative and asked him for an appointment. He pressured me to explain why—I doubt he asked the same of my classmates when they made an appointment. Professor Mathis made me feel like I was a lost case, undeserving of his time and attention.

When we met, I explained that I was formally educated in my native land and that I was merely experiencing a temporary language barrier. After the meeting, I noticed he started showing some level of human compassion toward me. He suggested that, instead of taking the required final test, I prepare a portfolio as the final project for his class, which would allow me to take English 102. He said he doubted I would pass that test; however, being resolute to prove him wrong, I studied as hard as possible and took the test, which I passed.

After I passed that test, moved to English 102, and graduated from the community college, I did not see Professor Mathis again for 11 years. I unexpectedly ran into Professor Mathis when he was visiting the University of Massachusetts at Amherst, where I was pursuing a doctorate degree. "Are you Professor Mathis?" I asked.

"Yes, I am," he said. "You're Pierre, right? Weren't you in my English class at Massachusetts Bay Community College?" I said that I was, and he asked what I was doing at the university.

"I am finishing a doctorate in education," I said.
In a surprised tone, he replied, "Oh, wow! Really? Good for you!"

I thanked him and asked what he was doing there. Reluctantly, he said, "I am considering applying for the doctoral program in the English Department here." We talked for a while and wished each other good luck as we said good-bye.

My experience with linguicism—that is, an " ideological construct that essentially involves the dominant group/language presenting an idealized image of itself, stigmatizing the dominated group/language, and rationalizing the relationship between the two, always to the advantage of the dominant group/language" (Phillipson, as cited in Macedo et al., 2003, p. 90)—tells me that racism and xenophobia are not isolated. Many People of Color, including highly respected professors of color, have had similar experiences. For example, Donaldo Macedo narrated a painful xenophobic, racist, and linguicist experience he had with a professor while he was a student. Macedo (1994) states:

> In September 1969, I euphorically began my studies at UMass/Boston. My enthusiasm was drastically short-lived because of my Freshman English professor, who, ironically, is a colleague of mine in the English Department where I teach today. This professor wanted us to read six novels and to keep a journal that we were to hand in at the end of the semester. The length, he emphasized, was to be forty-five pages. After the second class, I went into his office and explained that I had been in the country a relatively short time and that my major goal was to learn how to write well in English so that I could succeed in my studies. I also told him that I had little difficulty understanding his lectures but found it more difficult to express myself in English. I asked if I could meet with him periodically to go over my journal assignment to guide me in the process. His guidance would not only teach me about the fundamentals of writing, but it would also allow me to avoid turning in a forty-five page journal written over a semester without any feedback in the interim. When I finished voicing my concerns, he professionally rose from the chair, adjusted his eyeglasses and said, "Sonny, you should go learn English, then come to take my class." (p. 2)

A very good old friend of mine experienced similar linguistic and racial discrimination at his workplace. Like me, my friend was born in Haiti and grew up there. He immigrated to the United States in 1993. He has two master's degrees, one in finance and the other in transportation management. He started law school but had to take some time off to concentrate on his position as the manager of finance at a company in New York City. I interviewed him for another book project about his experience and changed his name there to Mario to protect his identity. He narrated his experience with linguicism and racism:

> Racism is a big issue in this country and I am exposed to it in school and at work. I was advised to change my major because of my accent. I wanted to major in English literature, but some of my professors advised me not to pursue a degree in English. They said that I was not going to be successful with it because of my accent. (Orelus, 2009, p. 188)

My racist and xenophobic experiences and those of Professor Macedo, my friend, and others show we have a long way to go before we can honestly and genuinely talk about democracy and social justice for black and brown people in this country. My painful experiences with my classmate Jennifer and Professor Mathis inspired me to pursue a master's degree in Applied Linguistics with a concentration in ESL, aiming to help immigrant children acquire English and critical thinking skills. While I was working on my master's degree and later on my doctoral degree, I had the privilege of being exposed to the scholarly work of, to be acquainted with and mentored by, and to take classes from and work with phenomenal scholars, such as Sonia Nieto, Donaldo Macedo, and Pepi Leistyna, who are deeply vested in culture and language issues. These scholars inspired me to explore these issues beyond the walls of the classroom. Since my graduate work, I have explored the history and politics of language in the United States and beyond. The knowledge I have acquired while exploring the literature on language issues has helped me understand the underlying reasons that may have led many to discriminate against those who speak hegemonic languages like English and French with a "foreign" accent.

Language is ideologically loaded and intrinsically connected to many forms of oppression, including racism. Macedo et al. (2003) call this connection "linguoracism." They argue "linguoracism more accurately names the insidious racism involved in all forms of linguistic imperialism" (p. 91). Language is also connected to social class and unequal power relations between racially and economically dominant groups as well as between dominant and subjugated languages. Historically, those in power have always attempted to force those in subordinate positions in society to speak and embrace their dominant culture and language. As wa Thiong'o eloquently pointed out in his book, *Decolonizing the Mind*, this form of oppression can be traced back to the colonial period within which the colonizers forced the colonized to speak their dominant languages (wa Thiong'o, 1986). This form of linguistic oppression has been revived in the so-called modern or postmodern time through Western neocolonial-language domestic and foreign policies, such the English-only movement in the United States (Macedo et al., 2003).

In the United States, for example, forcing minoritized people to speak English at the expense of their native languages is, in my view, a neocolonial form of linguistic domination. Invading and occupying countries and expecting the people in the occupied lands to speak the invaders' and occupiers' language and embrace their Western lifestyle is a renewed form of colonialism disguised with a different mask (Macedo et al., 2003; Phillipson, 1992; Pennycook, 2001). Finally, preventing minoritized students from speaking and embracing their own language(s) for fear they would not be fully integrated in the dominant culture is a way of colonizing their minds and souls (wa Thiong'o, 1986). There is no other name for this form of domination but "linguistic imperialism" (Phillipson, 1992, 2010). Racial and linguistic discrimination is a daily reality for many people of color, including myself, as they continue both their professional and academic journey here in the United States.

Lessons Learned from My Personal and Professional Journey

In my experience, both as a student and as a professor, I have learned that highly dedicated students and professors of color are discriminated against because of their racial and linguistic backgrounds and nationalities. For example, I have always had to prove my intelligence and intellectual ability, especially because I refuse to be unfairly and incorrectly labeled as the beneficiary of affirmative action, although many are aware that white women have benefited more from this law than People of Color have. Challenging this prejudicial assumption about minorities, Carlos Munoz, a university professor of color stated, "Minority job applicants must be superstars to be able to say that 'now you can't deny that I am qualified'" (as cited in Schneider, 1998, p. 11).

Of course I am not the only person being targeted because of my racial and linguistic background. Other professors of color have also been victims of individual and institutional racism. For example, the distinguished U.S. legal scholar Richard Delgado has faced racial invisibility with some of his white colleagues. According to Delgado, "Many of my White colleagues do not really know what a Latino is. Others know, but barely tolerate me, even though I am one of the top legal publishers in the country and well liked by my students" (as cited in Orelus, 2011b, p. 11). Professor Delgado has also experienced racial discrimination, such as racial profiling. He narrates how he was racially profiled while traveling back home from an academic conference he attended:

> Even dignified, well-dressed professionals encounter police profiling and challenges at work. I've been stopped by university police merely for looking out of place in the law building during evening hours. The incident has nothing to do with my income or class, but with my color and race. On other occasions, highway police have pulled me over just to check me out, even though I was driving a sober-looking rental car sedately and on my way back from an academic conference. (as cited in Orelus, 2011b, p. 12)

Likewise, Sharon Subreenduth (2008), a South African professor of color teaching at Bowling Green State University, faced similar xenophobic and racial discriminations. In a narrative essay, "Deconstructing the Politics of a Differently Colored Transnational Identity," Subreenduth describes how a white American senior researcher dismissed and stripped her of her South African identity and her commitments to conduct research in her native land, South Africa. The white senior researcher had done some research in South Africa and represented himself as an expert in South Africa's history, culture, and politics, while representing Subreenduth, a junior faculty member, as the "other." Not surprisingly, Subreenduth was unhappy with the way the white senior researcher treated her:

> Ironically, the senior researcher claims authority about (more authentically) knowing about South Africa and I became the "othered" both in South Africa and in the U.S. By virtue of the senior researcher's self-referential claims, probably by our existence within the imperial logic of global racial dynamics and hierarchy, the senior researcher became the authorized person to speak for and on behalf of South African issues, and thus became the legitimate researcher in the U.S. and S.A. (p. 50)

Drawing on her painful experience with the white American researcher, Subreenduth (2008) suggests that, "In order to rupture the underpinnings of oppression, one needs to counter and disrupt the operation of othering and objectification within academia and academic spaces" (p. 43). Similarly, Zeus Leonardo, a professor at University of California at Berkeley, who was born in the Philippines but grew up in the United States, critically described and analyzed how professors of color, including himself, have faced and resisted racial marginalization in the U.S. academy. Leonardo (2011) contends:

> The academy is so racial and precisely racializing that many scholars of color feel under siege and constantly under the White gaze. Some of us react with a heightened sense of embattlement, which affects our sense of equilibrium. Some even begin to think that *they are the problem*, and Du Bois' question of "How does it feel to be a problem?" becomes their mantra. They may assume qualities they have always disliked in other people: suspiciousness, negativity, even pessimism. Becoming embattled is a downward spiral as it begins to gnaw away at their ability to maintain good relationships with colleagues. It begins to affect their emotional and mental well-being. This is not their fault and even less their doing. But it reminds us that we must find a collective way to deal with the alienation that scholars of color experience in the academy like an illness that threatens personal and collective development. (as cited in Orelus, 2011b, p. 32)

Certainly, the examples given are only a few among many. Countless similar examples can be given to further illustrate how those in powerful positions in the U.S. academy often use the racial, ethnic, and linguistic backgrounds of professors of color to marginalize them, as well as how such treatment has negatively impacted their identities and material conditions. The key point that needs to be emphasized is that a person cannot and should not detach one form of oppression from another, for all forms of oppression are interconnected. In other words, racism, linguicism, and xenophobia, among others, are interrelated and, therefore, should not be analyzed separately; they all need to be part of the larger discussion and analysis of social injustice facing People of Color in the West and beyond.

Although my narrative reflects, first and foremost, my long personal and professional struggles to affirm my multiple identities in a so-called U.S. democratic land, it also reflects the stories shared by many People of Color. Lee Anne Bell (2010) states:

> As we link our individual stories into a collective story we discern patterns of racism. We see how dominance and subordination are engendered, even against our desires. We witness how or stories are interconnected, how advantage and disadvantage are constructed. (p. 51)

I argue that stories like mine, as well as those of other oppressed groups, need to be told as counter narratives to grand narratives, which mainly reflect the voice of dominant groups. The authentic voice of those who have been marginalized can be genuinely heard through their own narratives but not through truncated versions of such narratives as reported in Western history textbooks. Bell continues:

> Through such renderings, the history presented by the dominant group is made to "seem transparent" and thus uncontestable, making it difficult for aggrieved communities to get their claims for justice recognized. In the face of "official memory" those who are marginalized must struggle to hold on to their own representations, and can flounder when there are no social mirrors that accurately and meaningfully reflect their experiences. A myopic focus on the present through the haze of a fixed and glorified past also means that the broader society is bereft of the kind of deep historical knowing that could make genuine progress on racial matters possible. (p. 47)

Conclusion

Ending this chapter, I emphasize that the narratives of many oppressed people that have been relegated to the periphery for decades must be written to challenge those in positions of power who have often labeled them as "story telling" or "too emotional." This dominant discourse only serves to perpetuate the primacy of Western grand narratives permeating most canonical texts. Counter narratives used as a form of inquiry to articulate a person's story with his or her dissident voice are a great step toward self-liberation, for a person's liberation lies in his or her dissident voice. I hope the stories shared in this chapter help raise racial and linguistic consciousness among people so they can align with and support marginalized Peoples of Color, including immigrants of color, in their struggles to defend their humanity against white supremacy and linguoracism.

Conclusion

Lessons Learned, Looking Forward

Linguoracism and white hegemony have much to do with the linguistic, racial, and socioeconomic marginalization of people of color, particularly those who are poor. Shedding some light on these issues is the overarching goal of this book. Despite the post-racial discourse circulated in the mainstream media, especially after Barack Obama was elected president in 2008 and re-elected in 2012, people of color have continued to face various forms of oppression.

As the narratives shaping the story line of this book illuminate, all forms of oppression are connected. For instance, looking at a person's race from a dominant, superior perspective *vis-à-vis* other races is no different from looking at a person's language from a hegemonic, superior standpoint in relation to other languages often labeled as inferior. Therefore, racial oppression should not be seen and treated as a more important social justice issue than linguistic domination.

To put emphasis on one form of oppression because it serves our interests and meets our needs and leaves others out because we assume they do not directly affect us is a deep revelation of our individualistic and self-serving approach of the world informed by the contour of our familial, educational, social, and political environments. These environments include the mainstream media, which have earned the reputation of distorting stories and misinforming viewers to continue serving the interests of the powerful, and schools in which students are often denied the knowledge of their history, prohibited from speaking their native tongue, feel isolated, excluded, and oppressed because of the way many teachers treat, misinform, and discriminate against them.

Simultaneously, it must be pointed out that schools can also be, and have been, a site of struggle and resistance in which a person can counter many forms of oppression occurring within. For example, social justice educators, teacher activists, and public intellectuals from different disciplines and foci, such as Jonathan Kozol, John Dewey, Paulo Freire, Antonia Darder, Sandy Grande, Gloria Watkins (bell hooks), Patricia H. Collins, Myriam Torres, Angela Valenzuela, Angela Davis, Sonia Nieto, Christine Sleeter, Peter McLaren, Pepi Leistyna, Paul Carr, George Sefa Dei, Ali Abdi, Marisol Ruiz, Curry Malott, Henry Giroux, Donaldo Macedo, Joe Kincheloe, and Stanley Aronowitz, have viewed and used schools as a site of struggle in which a person can resist inequality and other forms of oppression occurring and affecting people, including parents and members of various communities, beyond the schoolyard. These educators, teachers, and scholars have challenged the oppressive, neoliberal, capitalist, and inequitable nature of the U.S. academy, making evident through their scholarly and activist work the linkages existing between schools, politics, and society and the ideological underpinning of these entities. Likewise, grassroots media like *DemocracyNow!* and *Link TV* have served as alternative tools to unveil misinformation and propaganda circulated through the corporate machine and the mainstream media, being sold as a commodity to the public.

These examples suggest a person should always be hopeful, even when in the midst of the worse form of adversity or confronting various forms of oppression like Whitecentricism, linguoracism, racism, and xenophobia, by which people of color, including immigrants of color, English language learners, and bilingual students, have been victimized. Losing hope should never be an option, especially for social justice-oriented teachers, progressive community organizers, and social and political activists who have been fighting against "savage inequalities" (Kozol, 1991) in schools and society at large and have been impacting linguistically, culturally, racially, and economically marginalized groups.

Just as people should not be discriminated against because of their race, gender, and sexuality, no one should be subjected to personal humiliation or attacks because of their non-dominant language and non-standard accent. Discriminating against someone because of his or her native tongue and accent is nothing but an assault on his or her sense of self and humanity, for people have no control over what languages they were born into and grew up speaking. Second language learners, including English language learners, do not have control over their non-native accents. If people are expected to learn or choose to learn a second or third language to communicate with people from different linguistic and racial backgrounds and nationality, why are they then punished for doing so?

In other words, is it fair that people have to pay a price for learning a second language to expand their linguistic repertoire to connect with others from various linguistic and cultural backgrounds? I find language- and accent-based discrimination unjust and absurd, as multilingualism and various forms of accents have fundamentally contributed to the beauty and advancement of the world. Likewise, it is inhuman to isolate and discriminate against someone because of his or her skin tone. Racial discrimination is as painful as language-, class-, and gender-based discrimination.

I cannot imagine how the world would be if there were only one language and one category of people living in it. If we were living in a world occupied by people of the same race and culture who speak the same language with the same accent, we would not then be talking about diversity, which has unfortunately become a meaningless word to many people, particularly those who have been historically marginalized. How can we honestly talk about diversity when people of other races constructed as inferior and who speak dominant languages, such as English and French with an accent different from the so-called standard accent have been discriminated against at school, work, and other places?

Likewise, how can we truthfully talk about social equality when people who hold key positions in society tend to belong only to the dominant racial and economic group? I argue that, for the world to be racially, linguistically, socially, and economically inclusive and fair, a profound institutional shift in many white, male- dominated Western countries, including the United States, the United Kingdom, and France, needs to happen. More specifically, institutions in these countries, such as the universities and colleges, the government, and the work place, need to create ample space for a diverse body of multilingual and multiracial individuals from different social classes, nationalities, and countries of origin as well as linguistic and religious backgrounds. My hope is that this book serves as an entry point into the debate around these issues as well as around issues concerning the need to work collectively to co-construct a society in which Whitecentrism, linguoracism, and other forms of oppression are eradicated.

Epilogue
The Unfinished Business of Decolonization: An Interview with Pierre Wilbert Orelus

Without a decolonizing mentality, smart students from disenfranchised backgrounds often find it difficult to succeed in the educational institutions of the dominator culture. This holds true even for those students who have embraced the values of the dominant culture. In fact, those students may be the least prepared for the barriers they face because they have so convinced themselves that they are different from other members of their group. (hooks, 2010, p. 26)

Every colonized people—in other words, every people in whose soul an inferiority complex has been created by the death and burial of its local cultural originality—finds itself face to face with the language of the "civilizing" nation; that is, with the culture of the mother country. The colonized is elevated above his "jungle" status in proportion to his adoption of the mother country's cultural standards. He becomes whiter as he renounces his blackness, his jungle. (Fanon, 1967, p. 18)

The domination of a people's language by the languages of the colonizing nations was crucial to the domination of the mental universe of the colonized. (wa Thiong'o, 1986, p. 16)

Context of Dialogue

This dialogue between Giuseppe de Simone, a doctoral student in Italy, and I took place in the fall of 2009, was originally conducted in French, and was later translated into English. It has been expanded since. To substantiate my arguments made throughout the dialogue, I drew on relevant literature. This dialogue focuses on important issues, such as colonialism, education, language, culture, and identity. Throughout this dialogue, I argue that colonialism has taken a different form and that its legacy continues to affect student learning and the school system in formerly colonized countries. Specifically, I contend that many students in formely colonized countries have been educated in and forced to embrace the language of the colonizer at the expense of their native tongues. Further, I maintain that this colonial legacy has affected the learning process of these students, arguing that the language in which students learn best is their native tongue. Finally, I make an appeal to counter the neocolonial cultural and linguistic influence of the West, while acknowledging the educational and intellectual importance of exchange of knowledge and culture between Westerners and non-Westerners.

The Dialogue

>Giuseppe de Simone: The colonial domination does not end with decolonization. What is the role of education in the fight against neocolonialism?

>Orelus: You ask me what should be the role of education in the fight against neocolonialism, right? I think that, at the school level, teachers should help students reach political consciousness concerning the sociopolitical situation of their countries; for example, in Haiti, there are students who don't understand the negative effects of colonialism on the school system of their country. I think it's very important that teachers help students understand the sociopolitical situation that not only affects their education but also the socioeconomic conditions of farmers, social workers, and factory workers. Unfortunately, there are teachers who are not conscious of colonial impacts on education, specifically on the school system of countries like Haiti and even the United States.

Students should know that the already inhabited territory that has become the United States was colonized by England, but some American students ignore this historical fact. For example, some 10 years ago or so, I started teaching at a high school; most of my students thought that countries that had been colonized were only African countries; they didn't think that the United States was also colonized. Educators should help students understand the history of colonialism and the colonial effects on the way these students think and act. The first step must be taken at the school level.

Giuseppe de Simone: So you think someone should teach them that the United States was also colonized. I am going to ask you a similar question. You know well the situation of the school system of a decolonized country like Haiti, as well as that of a colonizing (and colonized) country like the United States. Is there, in the school system of the United States, a memory of the colonial past? Or has the past been erased in people's memory? Has it been taught to students in the United States that this country has colonized countries in the Americas like Haiti?

Orelus: That's what I've just said. I don't want to generalize on the American situation, because maybe there are some students who know the United States was colonized; I had American students who didn't know that the United States was colonized by England. That's why many are unaware of the colonial effect on a formerly colonized country and people; they don't think like you and I or other people do who are fully aware of this colonial legacy.

Giuseppe de Simone: What is the best language of instruction to teach students in colonized states? Should a person use the language of the colonizer or the indigenous language?

Orelus: I think it's important to know more than one language. Personally, I am not against learning and speaking colonizers' languages, because knowing more than one language is an advantage in that it enables a person to communicate with people from diverse linguistic and cultural backgrounds. More specifically, speaking multiple languages puts a person in a unique position to know more about other cultures, because language is intrinsically linked to culture. For example, if I speak Italian, this linguistic ability and knowledge might help me have a better sense of Italian culture, but the problem I have with colonizers is that they have tried to impose their languages on colonized people at the expense of the native tongues of the latter. They think that the colonized should embrace and maintain the language of the colonizers. During the colonial period, the colonizers forced the colonized to embrace the culture of the colonizers. For example, in Haiti, students are forced to learn in French at the expense of their native language, Creole. I think both languages should be used.

In other words, the Haitian Creole and French should be used simultaneously as language of instruction at the K-12 and university levels, since many Haitians, including myself, believe that Haiti is a bilingual society. Haiti is indeed a bilingual country. However, the problem is that the Creole language is not as valued as French, which is the language we have inherited from the French colonizers. Many Haitians that I know, including some family members, sadly believe that French is superior to Creole, the native language of the poor working class Haitians. These Haitians would sacrifice a lot to send their children to private schools in which French is the language of instruction, even when they can't speak, or can't speak well, French. This is a very complicated and negative colonial legacy Haiti has yet to overcome, as I noted earlier.

Now to respond directly to your question. I would say that I don't believe it's a question of *what language must be adopted.* The fundamental question a person should ask him- or herself is: *What is the language in which students learn best?* In my view, Creole, the native language of Haitians, should be the language of instruction. For example, you are Italian. In what language do you learn best? I think the language in which you can learn comfortably is in your native language, that is, your mother's and father's tongue. If, as a colonizer, I try to impose the English or the French language on you, you would experience many learning problems, including linguistic problems. But if you're given the opportunity to learn in your native language, it will be much easier for you to learn. So I would say it's much better for students to use their native language to learn. This will certainly facilitate their learning process.

Allow me to share further with you my experience with linguistic and cultural colonialism in Haiti as a student. For example, in my native country, Haiti, even after 200 years of independence, the language of the French colonizers is still valued over the Haitian native language, Creole. When I was in middle school and high school (from the mid-1980s to the early 1990s), all of the textbooks that I had to use for class were in French. Nowhere in these textbooks, either on the cover or inside, were there pictures that reflected the reality of Haiti. These textbooks were, and perhaps still are, a reflection of the cultural and historical realities of France, realities to which Haitian students like myself could not relate. As a result, a great number of Haitian students, including myself, felt linguistically and culturally homeless, because there was no connection between what we read in these textbooks and our culture. In fact, as a high school student, I always felt foreign and culturally and historically alienated reading stories in these textbooks, whose cultural and historical baggage was irrelevant to my lived experience. This is well captured by Kempf and Dei (2006), who eloquently argues that, "When students see neither themselves nor their histories reflected in their education, disengagement understandably follows" (p. 132).

Like Kempf and Dei observe, not being able to see myself culturally and historically through school materials that my teacher used in class led me to resist what he taught in class. This also led me to question my mathematics teacher's attitude toward the French language and culture. This teacher always took pride in recounting how well French educators trained him to become a math teacher at a French Teacher Training Program in Haiti. At no time did he ever use in class a single word of Creole, the language I knew best as a working class student. Instead, he seemed to take pride in using French as the language of instruction.

Moreover, throughout my high school experience in Haiti, I was never encouraged by my teachers to challenge and try to deconstruct the hidden ideology embedded in textbooks imported from France that I was required to use in class. On the contrary, what I witnessed and personally experienced was that teachers were not only complacent about teaching French literature and history, but they also took pride in repeating, like parrots, to students their pre-fabricated knowledge about these subjects. At no time, did I recall my high school teachers attempting to question and challenge Western values, beliefs, and ideology entrenched in French textbooks that were imposed on them to use in class. Consequently, Haitian students, including myself, spent years from elementary to middle and high schools absorbing information that had no meaning to their lives. In fact, information acquired from these textbooks structured my mind, to a great extent, to accept passively and reproduce the false idea that France is Haiti's mother country and source of knowledge.

After years of indoctrination, I became a docile reproducer of French Western values, beliefs, and cultural norms. For instance, until I developed critical consciousness, I used to believe that the French language and literature were better than Creole and the Haitian literature. As a result, through social interaction, I always used French, the language of the colonizer, to communicate with and impress people, rather than Creole, my native tongue. What I was not aware of, then, as Wane (2006) notes, was that:

> The use of a foreign language as a medium of education makes a child foreign within her or his own culture, environment, etc. This creates a colonial alienation. What is worse, the neocolonized subject is made to see the world and where she or he stands in it as seen, and defined by or reflected in the culture of the language

of imposition. This is made worse when the neocolonized subject is exposed to images of her or his world mirrored in the written language of her or his colonizer, where the natives' language, cultures, history, or people are associated with low status, slow intelligence, and barbarism. (p. 100)

Wane's remark speaks directly to my schooling experience in Haiti. Reflecting on that experience, I have come to understand that teachers or students, who lack historical and cultural consciousness, sometimes let themselves get trapped in the linguistic oppression of the colonizers, who always expect the colonized to speak the colonial language at the expense of their own. This sad experience with my math teacher, more importantly, helped me better understand that the school system of a country constitutes its ideological apparatus. Therefore, if any radical social, cultural, and political changes are to occur, it must begin in the school system that has historically been used to maintain and/or challenge the status quo. It goes without saying that the school system can be a dangerous institution that reproduces the dominant ideology and/or a site of struggle in which ideological and political fights for a just and democratic society can take place.

Furthermore, looking back at my schooling experience in Haiti, I now realize how sad it is that most of my high school classmates were more knowledgeable about French literature and history than they were about Haitian literature and culture. This is precisely what happened to colonized people during colonization. The colonized were more knowledgeable about the culture and history of the colonizer than their own. However, this did not happen in a vacuum, as Semali and Kincheloe (1999) made clear in their book, *What Is Indigenous Knowledge? Voices from the Academy*. Kincheloe and Semali maintain that the colonized, through schooling, were taught that their indigenous knowledge was barbarous, uncivilized, and, therefore, worthless in comparison to the European-based knowledge and formation they were receiving in school.

Linking Kincheloe and Semali's argument to the Haitian school system that I knew as a high school student, I argue that it was set up in a way that failed Haitian students both culturally and historically. In other words, this school system graduated students who might not have had a clear sense of their history and culture. Hence, locating this form of mis-education that my classmates and I experienced in a global educational context, I ask: What can be expected of a generation that does not to have a sound understanding of its own history and culture? I go further, asking: What should educators do to ensure that the school system of their countries is not a duplicate of the old colonial school system and/or the Western neoliberal educational policies?

A student's native tongue is the language in which he or she can easily make connections with his or her own culture and the world. It is important to mention something about speaking a language with a distinct accent, because having an accent matters across all languages. For example, I remember how frustrated I got with my accent in the English language when I was working on my bachelors, master's, and doctorate degrees. I continue to be annoyed with people constantly asking me where I am from based on my accent. Moreover, after being away from my native land for 9 years, I was extremely happy to return home to visit family members and friends, only to be told during my very first day there that I speak Creole with a funny accent and that I use too many English words while speaking. It is true that I unintentionally used some English words while speaking my native language, Creole, with friends and family members, but I never thought that my compatriots would see me through a different linguistic lens to the point at which they made a clear distinction between me, who had been living abroad for almost 20 years, and Haitians who had not left the island.

Likewise, although I am a U.S. naturalized citizen and have been living in the United States for about 2 decades, people still remind me that I am a stranger of some kind based on the types of questions they ask me about my accent when interacting with them. As soon as I open my mouth, the first question they usually ask me is, "Where are you from? You have an accent." It is not only people whose English is their native tongue who have asked me this question but also people with a distinctly non-native accent. Interestingly enough, I have been asked this type of question whether I am speaking Creole, English, Spanish, or French. For example, when I meet and speak in French with someone who is from a French-speaking country, especially France and Belgium, I am always asked where my accent is from. Likewise, when I speak Spanish with native Spanish speakers, I have received the same question. Sadly, although I was born and grew up in Haiti, Haitians living in the island often remind me when I visit family and friends that I speak Creole with some kind of foreign accent. From these three linguistic experiences, I have concluded that I speak four languages, Haitian Creole, French, English, and Spanish, with some kind of foreign accent. So, in some way, I am the accent guy when I speak, regardless of the language I am expressing myself in. I have accepted this identity marker, although, at times, it feels like a shadow that follows every step I make and every word I utter.

>Giuseppe de Simone: Your experience with the accent issue is interesting, to say the least. Going back to the language issues, I concur with you. That is, Creole should also be incorporated in the Haitian school curricu-

lum; for example, Creole should be taught both at K-12 and the university level, and research should be done in Creole. Shouldn't it be?

Orelus: I totally agree with you. Yes, Creole should be used at all levels. There are Haitian educators who are incorporating the Creole language at the university level. For example, when I was in college (I started college in Haiti, but I did not complete it there), I had a professor who only used Creole as the language of instruction, and he was harshly criticized for doing so. In Haiti, there exist places where a person feels he or she has to speak French to convince people that he or she is educated. If, for instance, a person is speaking French, people tend to assume that person is educated, whereas if a person is speaking Creole, people assume the opposite. That's where the problem lies. But I must tell you that things have changed since I left Haiti in the 1990s; there are many books written in Creole, and many teachers use these books to teach students, but French is still more valued than Creole. The French colonial legacy has much to do with this.

What many people, including many Haitians, fail to understand is that language is one of the most frequently recurring topics, often surfacing in debates centered on school reforms and the academic achievement of students, particularly linguistically, culturally, and marginalized students, who are often discriminated against in schools because of their language and culture. Most importantly, language shapes almost every facet of our lives, although many of us sometimes might take it for granted. Culturally, historically, politically, and ideologically, language is loaded. Historically, language has been used to liberate and oppress people at the same time. As a prime example, during colonization, the colonizers used their languages to oppress colonized people by imposing their languages, cultures, and histories on the colonized. They hired teachers who were submissive and loyal to the colonial regime to brainwash colonized students by making them believe that whatever is European or from Europe is better. In other contexts, languages have been used to pass on traditions, cultural, and religious and moral values and rituals to younger generations. People have used languages to communicate and connect with people from other cultural, racial, and socio-economic backgrounds. In short, besides shaping our identity, language has enabled us to transcend many socio-cultural barriers. Despite all of these sociological, historical, cultural, educational, and psychological facts about language, many still ignore the importance of this important medium and tool in a person's academic, professional, and personal successes. However, those who are in powerful positions to dominate, control, and oppress others are fully aware of these facts. This is precisely why they have tried to promote the use of certain languages in public, private, and political spheres, while attempting to oppress other languages and the people who speak them. This is not a coincidence, nor is it an innocent act. It is ideologically, politically, and economically motivated.

> Giuseppe de Simone: According to your experience, how is the cultural domination in schools made possible? There is, for instance, authoritarianism of teachers and the culture composed of memorizing notions. What are the other instruments of the postcolonial domination in schools?

> Orelus: I think teachers should create a classroom environment in which students can freely express their ideas. They should engage in a dialogue with students. Unfortunately, in certain school environments, teachers don't encourage students to express their opinion, let alone take a position that may challenge the teacher's position on some issues. For example, at many institutions at which I studied and taught, there were many professors who were very traditional and seemed threatened when students challenged them. It seemed they felt personally attacked when students asked pertinent questions about the issues they were trying to address in their classes. I think the first step that should be taken should be to create a classroom environment in which students can freely express their ideas and take positions that might be different from those of their professors or teachers. The classroom should be a democratic pedagogical place in which both students and teachers should challenge one another and agree or disagree on issues, including heated issues like the war in Iraq, the Israeli and Palestinian conflict, and immigrant, gay, women's, and worker's rights.

Moreover, I think professors should help students value their cultural heritage. There are students who have been told directly or indirectly that their culture is inferior. Therefore, I think helping students develop some consciousness of their cultural value is very important. Unfortunately, in some school environments, many professors fail to do so. Helping students develop cultural consciousness is fundamental as far as education is concerned, for lacking a solid knowledge of one's own culture is very problematic in the sense that it can be detrimental to a person's academic and political growth. In my opinion, cultural knowledge is liberatory and political. What a person should do is to begin valorizing his or her own culture, for, by having a historical knowledge of his or her own culture, he or she can fight against the influence of the United States', England's, and France's imperialism.

> Giuseppe de Simone: In my dissertation, I argue that, ultimately, postcolonial education should be intercultural. In your opinion, what should be the goal of postcolonial education? Should it be intercultural?
>
> Orelus: What do you mean by "interculture" in this context?
>
> Giuseppe de Simone: I want to say that the reconstruction of colonial significances should take into account other cultures and that a person shouldn't have a narrowed view about the world. Interculture meaning accepting other cultures and projecting the future with them.
>
> Orelus: As you know, a person lives in a connected world. A person cannot isolate him- or herself from other cultures and other countries. I think it is important that we embrace other cultures, but this does not mean that someone should abandon his or her own culture to embrace another. I think it's important, for example, to use cultural elements from the United States and France that can be valuable, but, at the same time, a person should take into account the extent to which cultural influence of other countries might affect the cultural life of others. If I can take Haiti, as an example, I would say that the United States has a lot of cultural influence on this country, but this cultural influence is not necessarily bad. There are some positive elements a person can use from it. For example, American music has a great influence on our music. Nowadays, Haitian youth no longer listen to French music. Instead, they listen to American music. Although they don't know the content of many American songs, they prefer embracing the American music. This type of influence can be positive or negative, depending on how this influence is received. It's totally impossible to live in an isolated way; whether a person likes it or not, there are other cultures that influence our society. Therefore, it's important to be aware of both the positive and the negative elements of these cultures.
>
> Giuseppe de Simone: So you think a person should be very careful when speaking of interculture, because it can be dangerous?
>
> Orelus: Yes, of course.
>
> Giuseppe de Simone: I studied postcolonial education in Africa. The colonization created a cultural alienation and has separated education from

experience. For example, a person learned the history of France and of Europe instead of learning the history of Africa and the African culture. After decolonization, the African response has been to close the gap between education and the lived experience of people. They have eliminated school manuals coming from Europe. They have also made schools function at a rural level; that is, schools have been transformed into agricultural communities in which someone would work more than study. But education is not only about experience, it's also abstraction; it's more than work and immediate experience. According to you, what is the relationship between education and experience?

Orelus: I would like to begin by giving you an example: There are countries that are not as "advanced" as others. There are African countries that are not as "advanced" as the United States and France. In these countries, there are many farmers who don't know how to read and write, but they have practical knowledge. I think this type of knowledge should be valorized. Unfortunately, there are intellectuals living in these countries whose minds have been colonized, who think the knowledge farmers and factory workers have is not valuable. Therefore, they have the tendency to valorize the abstract knowledge they received from canonical European texts pervasive in many schools. Most of these intellectuals had been educated in the West; when they go back to their country, they don't take into account the practical knowledge that workers and farmers have. They think that workers should think like them. I think that both types of knowledge are valuable. A person should have access to academic knowledge, but, at the same time, a person should recognize that farmers have their own knowledge based on practical experiences, and this form of knowledge should be incorporated in the school curriculum as well. So I don't believe it should be a question of *what is the most valuable knowledge?* I think both types of knowledge are valuable. But, as I told you, in countries that had been colonized, intellectuals have the tendency to think that the type of knowledge that workers and peasants have is not valuable, and I think it's a colonial tendency of which they should get rid.

Giuseppe de Simone: What is important is not to reduce all knowledge, all sorts of education to farming education, or all education to academic knowledge, but rather respect all forms of education?

Orelus: Absolutely! All forms of knowledge are valuable and, therefore, should be embraced and respected.

Giuseppe de Simone: In Africa after the 1960s, they've tried to eradicate illiteracy by valuing the agricultural and farming communities. However, no attention was paid at the secondary or university level. It was a problem, because there was no research done regarding the adequate formation of teachers. I think both should go hand in hand. Otherwise, the school system is going to be affected.

Orelus: Yes, I agree with you. The colonial influence on countries that had been colonized has always been strong; therefore, people should continue to fight the cultural influence of Western countries like the United States, France, England, and Portugal. It's really a complex issue. That's the reason there isn't *a* solution to this problem. People should take into account the socioeconomic and political factors that affect *the way a person thinks and sees the world.*

Giuseppe de Simone: How is it possible to encounter structures of economic, political, and pedagogical dominations quite similar even among very distant nations located in different continents?

Orelus: That's a very good question. But what a person should know is that, for example, like Senegal, Haiti was colonized by France. It's the same colonizers who colonized these two countries. That's why a person finds many similarities between Senegal and Haiti and other countries that France colonized. That's simple. The geographical location has nothing to do with the cultural influence Western colonizing countries have had on countries they colonized. When I meet people from Senegal or from Martinique, in some way, they think like some Haitians, because they were also colonized by the French. The colonial legacy has similar effects on the minds of those who have been colonized. However, to avoid generalization about these countries, which can be very dangerous and counterproductive, I must add that a person should always take into account the particular historical, cultural, and political context of these countries, despite the similar colonial legacy they all share. Do you understand what I mean?

Giuseppe de Simone: Yes, that's quite clear. Another question: In your book, *Education Under Occupation,* you draw on the scholarly work of a Western scholar, John Dewey. Do you think it's possible to deconstruct colonial knowledge by using theories coming from the West or should we use new theoretical framework that has nothing to do with the Western culture?

Orelus: That's a very good question. But listen, John Dewey was not a colonizer. The United States is an imperialist country that has occupied other countries, isn't it? But there are American scholars who are against American imperialism. Dewey was an American; however, his way of conceiving the world is appealing to me as a non-Westerner. That's why people, including myself, feel they can relate to Dewey's work. I am going to give you another example: There are many progressive and radical American scholars who are alive. Noam Chomsky is a prime example. He is American, isn't he? But his way of seeing the world goes beyond the U.S. borders. In fact, throughout his career, he has taken some radical positions against U.S. foreign policies about developing countries particularly. He has taken firm positions against U.S. imperialism. Chomsky understands fairly well the neocolonial situation of countries that had been colonized, such as Haiti. So he does not have a narrowed view of the world. The fact that a scholar is American does not mean this person can't understand the sociopolitical situation of formerly colonized countries. Throughout my writing, I draw on the scholarly work of both progressive Western and non-Western thinkers, such as Noam Chomsky, Howard Zinn, Peter McLaren, Paulo Freire, bell hooks, Sonia Nieto, Stuart Hall, Molefi Asante, Cornel West, Patricia Hill Collins, Antonia Darder, Edward Said, and, my intellectual hero, Frantz Fanon. These scholars have cultivated a passion for humanity and do not have a nationalist nor a narrowed idea of the world. This is why I have much appreciation for their work.

Bibliography

Abdi, A. A. (2005). Reflections on the long struggle for inclusion: The experiences of peoples of African origin. In W. Tettey & P. Puplampu (Eds.), *Negotiating identity and belonging: The African diaspora in Canada* (pp. 49–59). Calgary, AB: University of Calgary Press.

Acuña, R. (2008). *Corridors of migration: The odyssey of Mexican laborers, 1600–1933.* Tucson, AZ: University of Arizona Press.

Acuña, R. (2010). *Occupied America: A history of Chicanos* (7th ed.). Upper Saddle River, NJ: Prentice Hall.

Ahmed, S. (2000). *Strange encounters: Embodied others in post-coloniality.* New York, NY: Routledge.

Aldama, A. (2001). *Disrupting savagism: Intersecting Chicana/o, Mexican immigrant, and Native American struggles for self-representation.* Durham, NC: Duke University Press.

Alexander, B. (2005). Performance ethnography: The reenacting and inciting of culture. In N. Denzin & Y. Lincoln (Eds.), *The Sage handbook of qualitative research* (3rd ed.) pp. 411–442). Thousand Oaks, CA: Sage Publications.

Alexander, M. (2010). *The new Jim Crow: Mass incarceration in the age of colorblindness.* New York, NY: The New Press.

Anzaldúa, G. (1990). How to tame a wild tongue. In R. Ferguson, M. Gever, T. Minh-Ha, & C. West (Eds.), *Out there: Marginalization and contemporary cultures* (pp. 24–44). Cambridge, MA: The MIT Press.

Anzaldúa, G. (2007). *Borderlands/La frontera: The new mestiza* (3rd ed.). San Francisco, CA: Aunt Lute Books.
Appiah, K. A. (2005). *The ethics of identity*. Princeton, NJ: Princeton University Press.
Aronowitz, S. (2006). *Left turn: Forging a new political future*. Boulder, CO: Paradigm Publishers.
Asante, M. (2011). *The African American people: A global history*. New York, NY: Routledge.
Auerbach, E. R. (1995). The politics of the ESL classroom: Issues of power in pedagogical choices. In J. W. Tollefson (Ed.), *Power and inequality in language education* (pp. 1–18). New York, NY: Cambridge University Press.
Austin, F. (2012). *For African Americans, 50 years of high unemployment*. Retrieved from http://www.epi.org/publication/african-americans-50-years-high-unemployment/
Baird, F., & Kaufmann, K. (2008). *From Plato to Derrida*. Upper Saddle River, NJ: Pearson Prentice Hall.
Bakhtin, M. (1986). *The dialogic imagination*. Austin, TX: University of Texas Press.
Bell, D. (1992). *Faces at the bottom of the well: The permanence of racism*. New York, NY: Basic Books.
Bell, D. (2009). Who's afraid of critical race theory? In E. Taylor, D. Gillborn, & G. Ladson-Billings (Eds.), *Foundations of critical race theory in education* (pp. 37–50). New York, NY: Routledge.
Bell, L. A. (2010). *Storytelling for social justice: Connecting narrative and the arts in antiracist teaching*. New York, NY: Routledge.
Biko, S. (2007). *I write what I like*. Chicago, IL: University of Chicago Press.
Bonilla-Silva, E. (2003). *Racism without racists: Color-blind racism and the persistence of racial inequality in the United States*. Lanham, MD: Rowman & Littlefield Publishers.
Bonilla-Silva, E. (2010). *Anything but racism: How social scientists limit the significance of race*. New York, NY: Routledge.
Bourdieu, P. (1990). *The logic of practice*. (Trans. R. Nice). Stanford, CA: Stanford University Press.
Bourdieu, P. (1991). *Language and symbolic power*. (Trans. G. Raymond & M. Adamso). Cambridge, UK: Polity Press.
Bourdieu, P. (1998). *Practical reason: On the theory of action*. Stanford, CA: Stanford University Press.
Byrd, A. D., & Tharps, L. I. (2001). *Hair story: Untangling the roots of black hair in America*. New York, NY: St. Martin's Press.
Cabral, A. (1973). *Return to the source: Selected speeches by Amílcar Cabral*. New York, NY: Monthly Review Press.
Carr, P. R. (2007). The whiteness of educational policymaking. In P. R. Carr & D. E. Lund (Eds.), *The great white North? Exploring whiteness, privilege and identity in education* (pp. 223–233). Rotterdam, The Netherlands: Sense Publishers.

Carr, P. R. (2011). The quest for a critical pedagogy of democracy. In C. Malott & B. Porfilio (Eds.), *Critical pedagogy in the twenty-first century: A new generation of scholars* (pp. 187–210). Charlotte, NC: Information Age Publishing.

Carr, P. R., & Lund, D. E. (2007). *The great white North? Exploring whiteness, privilege and identity in education.* Rotterdam, The Netherlands: Sense Publishers.

Castells, M. (2006). *The power of identity* (Vol. 2). (2nd ed.). Malden, MA: Blackwell.

Césaire, A. (1972). *Discourse on colonialism.* New York, NY: Monthly Review Press.

Chomsky, N. (1994). *Secrets, lies and democracy.* Berkeley, CA: Odonian Press.

Chomsky, N. (2002). *Media control: The spectacular achievements of propaganda.* New York, NY: Seven Stories Press.

Chomsky, N. (2004). *Hegemony or survival: America's quest for global dominance.* New York, NY: Holt Paperbacks.

Chomsky, N. (2007). *Failed states: The abuse of power and the assault on democracy.* New York, NY: Holt Paperbacks.

Churchill, W. (2004). *Kill the Indian, save the man: The genocidal impact of American Indian residential schools.* San Francisco, CA: City Lights Books.

Coloma, R. S. (2008). Border crossing subjectivities and research: Through the prism of feminists of color. *Race, Ethnicity, and Education, 11*(1), 11–27.

Cook, M. (2005). *A brief history of the human race.* New York, NY: W. W. Norton & Company.

Crawford, J. (1991). *Bilingual education: History, politics, theory and practice* (2nd ed.). Los Angeles, CA: Bilingual Educational Services.

Crawford, J. (2008). *Advocating for English learners: Selected essays.* New York, NY: Multilingual Matters, Ltd.

Crenshaw, K. (1993). Mapping the margins: Intersectionality, identity politics, and violence against women of color. *Stanford Law Review, 43*(6), 1241–1299.

Cummins, J. (2000). *Language, power and pedagogy: Bilingual children in the crossfire.* Tonawanda, NY: Multilingual Matters, Ltd.

Darder, A. (2011). *A dissident voice: Essays on culture, pedagogy, and power.* New York, NY: Peter Lang Publishing.

Darder, A. (2012). *Culture and power in the classroom: Educational foundations for the schooling of bicultural students.* Boulder, CO: Paradigm Publishers.

De Tocqueville, A. (Grant, S.) (2000). *Democracy in America.* Indianapolis, IN: Hackett Publishing Company, Inc.

Dei, G. J. S. (1996). *Anti-racism education: Theory and practice.* Halifax, NS: Fernwood Publishing Co.

Dei, G. J. S. (1999). Knowledge and politics of social change: The implication of anti-racism. *British Journal of Sociology of Education, 20*(3), 395–409.

Dei, G. J. S. (2007). Foreword. In P. R. Carr & D. E. Lund (Eds.), *The great white North? Exploring whiteness, privilege and identity in education* (pp. vii–xii). Rotterdam, The Netherlands: Sense Publishers.

Dei, G. J. S. (2009). Afterword. The anti-colonial theory and the questions of survival and responsibility. In A. Kempf (Ed.), *Breaching the colonial contract: Anti-colonialism in the US and Canada* (pp. 251–254). New York, NY: Springer Press.

Dei, G. J. S. (2012). *Teaching Africa: Towards a transgressive pedagogy.* New York: Springer.

Dei, G. J. S., Karumanchery, L., & Karumanchery-Luik, N. (2004). *Playing the race card: Exposing white power and privilege.* New York, NY: Peter Lang Publishing.

Delgado, R. (1989). Storytelling for oppositionists and others: A plea for narrative. *Michigan Law Review, 87,* 2411–2441.

Delgado, R. (2011). Unveiling majoritarian myths and tales about race and racism: A conversation with Richard Delgado. In P. Orelus (Ed.), *Rethinking race, class, language, and gender. A dialogue with Noam Chomsky and other leading scholars* (pp. 7–15). Lanham, MD: Rowman & Littlefield Publishers.

Delgado, R., & Stefancic, J. (1995). *Critical race theory: The cutting edge.* Philadelphia, PA: Temple University Press.

Denzin, N. K. (2009). Critical pedagogy and democratic life or a radical democratic pedagogy. *Cultural Studies-Critical Methodologies, 9*(3), 379–397.

Dewey, J. (1997). *Democracy and education.* New York, NY: Free Press.

Dillard, C. (2006). *On spiritual strivings: Transforming an African American woman's academic life.* Albany: State University of New York Press.

Dillard, C. (2012). *Learning to (re) member the things we've learned to forget: Endarkened feminisms, spirituality, and the sacred nature of research and teaching.* New York, NY: Peter Lang Publishing.

Diop, C.A., (1974). *The African origin of civilization: Myth or reality.* (Trans. by Mercer Cook). New York, NY: Lawrence Hill & Co.

Douglass, F. (2012). *Narratives of the life of Frederick Douglass, an American slave.* New York, NY: Simon & Brown.

Du Bois, W. E. B (1995). *The souls of black folk.* New York, NY: Penguin Press.

Ellis, C. (2004). *The ethnography 1: A methodological novel about teaching and doing autoethnography.* Walnut Creek, CA: AltaMira.

Fairlie, R., & Sundstrom, W. (1999). The emergence, persistence, and recent widening of the racial unemployment gap. *Industrial and Labor Relations Review, 52*(2), 252–270.

Fanon, F. (1963). *The wretched of the earth.* New York, NY: Grove Press.

Fanon, F. (1965). *A dying colonialism.* New York, NY: Grove Press.

Fanon, F. (1967). *Black skin, white masks.* New York, NY: Grove Press.

Fedigan, J. (Director). (2010). *The angry heart: The impact of racism on heart disease among African Americans* [Motion picture], United States.

Firmin, A. (2000). *The equality of human races: Positivist anthropology.* (Trans. Asselin Firmin). Chicago, IL: University of Illinois Press.

Foucault, M. (1980). Two lectures. In C. Gordon (Ed.). *Power/knowledge: Selected interviews & other writings.* New York, NY: Pantheon Books.

Foucault, M. (1995). *Discipline and punish: The birth of the prison.* (Trans. Alan Sheridan). New York, NY: Vintage Books.

Freire, P. (1993). *Pedagogy of the oppressed.* (Trans. M. Ramos). New York, NY: The Continuum International Publishing Group.

Freire, P. (2005). *Teachers as cultural workers: Letters to those who dare teach.* Boulder, CO: Westview Press.

Gillborn, D. (2005). Education as an act of white supremacy: Whiteness, critical race theory and education reform. *Journal of Education Policy, 20*(4), 485–505.

Gillborn, D. (2008). *Racism and education: Coincidence or conspiracy?* London, England: Routledge.

Giroux, H. (2003). *The abandoned generation: Democracy beyond the culture of fear.* New York, NY: Palgrave Macmillan, Ltd.

Giroux, H. (2007). Democracy, education, and the politics of critical pedagogy. In P. McLaren & J. Kincheloe (Eds.), *Critical pedagogy: Where are we now?* (pp. 1–5). New York, NY: Peter Lang Publishing.

Giroux, H. (2012). *Disposable youth: Racialized memories, and the culture of cruelty.* New York, NY: Routledge.

Gobineau, A. (2010). *The inequality of human races.* Charleston, SC: Babu Press.

Gramsci, A. (1971). *Selections from the prison notebooks.* New York, NY: International Publishers.

Grande, S. (2004). *Red pedagogy: Native American social and political thought.* Lanham, MD: Rowman & Littlefield Publishers.

Grant, K., & Sleeter, C. (2007). *Turning on learning: Five approaches for multicultural teaching plans for race, gender and disability* (4th ed.). Hoboken, NJ: John Wiley & Sons, Inc.

Greene, M. (2009). In search of a critical pedagogy. In A. Darder, M. P. Baltodano, & R. D. Torres (Eds.), *The critical pedagogy reader* (2nd ed.). New York, NY: Routledge.

Hall, S. (Ed.) (1997). *Representation: Cultural representations and signifying practices.* London, UK: Sage Publications, Ltd.

Hamzeh, M. (2012). *Pedagogies of deveiling: Muslim girls & the hijab discourse.* Charlotte, NC: Information Age Publishing.

Harris, C. (1993). "Bell's blues." *University of Chicago Law Review, 60*(568): 783–93.

Herrnstein, J. R., & Murray, C. (1996). *The bell curve: Intelligence and class structure in American life.* New York, NY: Free Press.

Hirsch, E. D., Jr. (1987). *Cultural literacy: What every American needs to know.* New York, NY: Vintage Books.

Holland, D., Lachicotte Jr., W., Skinner, D., & Cain, C. (2003). *Identity and agency in cultural worlds.* Cambridge, MA: Harvard University Press.

Holman Jones, S. (2005). Autoethnography: Making the personal political. In N. Denzin & Y. Lincoln (Eds.), *The Sage handbook of qualitative research* (3rd ed., pp. 411–442). Thousand Oaks, CA: Sage Publications.

hooks, b. (1984). *Feminist theory: From margin to center.* Boston, MA: South End Press.

hooks, b. (1989). *Talking back: Thinking feminist, thinking black.* Boston, MA: South End Press.

hooks, b. (1992a). *Black looks: Race and representation*. Boston, MA: South End Press.
hooks, b. (1992b). *Teaching to transgress: Education as the practice of freedom*. New York, NY: Routledge.
hooks, b. (1994). *Teaching to Transgress: Education as the practice of freedom*. New York: Routledge.
hooks, b. (2010). *Teaching critical thinking: Practical wisdom*. New York, NY: Routledge.
Husband, T. (2007). Always black, always male: Race/cultural recollections and the qualitative researcher. Unpublished paper presented at the Congress of Qualitative Inquiry, May 3–6, University of Illinois, Champaign-Urbana.
Hutardo, A. (1996). *The color of privilege: Three blasphemies on race and feminism*. Michigan: The University of Michigan Press.
Jensen, A. R. (1969). How much can we boost IQ and scholastic achievement? *Harvard Educational Review, 39*, 1–123.
Jensen, R. (2005). *The heart of whiteness: Confronting race, racism, and white privilege*. San Francisco, CA: City Lights Books.
Kempf, A., & Dei, G. S. (2006). Anti-colonial historiography: Interrogating colonial education. In G. S. Dei & A. Kempf (Eds.), *Anti-colonialism and education: The politics of resistance*. Rotterdam/Taipei: Sense Publishers.
Kendall, F. (2012). *Understanding White privilege: Creating pathways to authentic relationships across race* (2nd edition). New York: Routledge.
Klein, N. (2007). *The shock doctrine: The rise of disaster capitalism*. New York, NY: Metropolitan Books.
Kneller, F. G. (1964). *Introduction to the philosophy of education*. New York, NY: John Wiley & Sons, Inc.
Kozol, J. (1985). *Death at an early age: The destruction of hearts and minds of Negro children in the Boston public schools*. New York, NY: Plume.
Kozol, J. (1991). *Savage inequalities: Children in America's schools*. New York, NY: Harper Perennial.
Kozol, J. (2006). *The shame of the nation: The restoration of apartheid schooling in America*. New York, NY: Crown Publishers.
Ladson-Billings, G. (2004). Just what is critical race theory and what's it doing in a nice field like education? In G. Ladson-Billings & D. Gillborn (Eds.), *The Routledge Falmer reader in multicultural education* (pp. 49–264). London, England: RoutledgeFalmer.
Lavia, J. (2006). The practice of postcoloniality: A pedagogy of hope. *Pedagogy, Culture & Society, 14*(3), 279–293.
Leistyna, P., & Alper, L. (2007). Critical media literacy for the 21st century: Taking our entertainment seriously. In D. Macedo & S. Steinberg(Eds.), *Media literacy: A reader* (pp. 54–78). New York, NY: Peter Lang Publishing.
Leonardo, Z. (Ed.). (2005). *Critical pedagogy and race*. Malden, MA: Wiley Blackwell Publishing.
Leonardo, Z. (2009). *Race, Whiteness, and education*. New York, NY: Routledge.

Leonardo, Z. (2011). Unmasking White supremacy and racism: A conversation with Zeus Leonardo. In P. Orelus (Ed.), *Rethinking race, class, language, and gender: A dialogue with Noam Chomsky and other leading scholars.* Lanham, MD: Rowman & Littlefield Publishers.

Linn, R. L. (2004). *Rethinking the No Child Left Behind Act accountability system.* Retrieved from www.cep-dc.org/pubs/Forum28July2004/

Lipman, P. (2004). *High stakes education: Inequality, globalization, and urban school reform.* New York, NY: Routledge.

Loewen, J. (1995). *Lies my teacher told me: Everything your American history textbook got wrong.* New York, NY: The New Press.

Loomba, A. (2002). *Colonialism/postcolonialism: The new critical idiom.* New York, NY: Routledge.

Lopez, A. (Ed.). (2005). *Post colonial Whiteness.* Albany, NY: State University of New York Press.

Macedo, D. (1994). *Literacies of power: What Americans are not allowed to know.* Boulder, CO: Westview Press.

Macedo, D. (2009). Unmasking prepackaged democracy. In S. Macrine (Ed.), *Critical pedagogy in uncertain times: Hopes and possibilities* (pp. 79–96). New York, NY: Palgrave Macmillan, Ltd.

Macedo, D., Dendrinos, B., & Gounari, P. (2003). *The hegemony of English.* Boulder, CO: Paradigm Publishers.

Macedo, D., & Steinberg, S. (2007). *Media literacy: A reader.* New York, NY: Peter Lang Publishing.

Marx, K. (1994). *The eighteenth brumaire of Louis Bonaparte.* New York, NY: International Publishers.

Matsuda, M. J., Lawrence, C., Delgado, R., & Crenshaw, K. W. (1993). *Words that wound: Critical race theory, assaultive speech, and the First Amendment.* Boulder, CO: Westview Press.

McIntosh, P. (1992). White privilege and male privilege: A personal account to see correspondences through work in women's studies. In M. Anderson & P. H. Collins (Eds.), *Race, class, and gender: An anthology* (pp. 70–81). Belmont, CA: Wadsworth Publishing.

McLaren, P. (1980). *Cries from the corridor.* London: Methuen.

McLaren, P. (2005). *Capitalists and conquerors: A critical pedagogy against empire.* Lanham, MD: Rowman & Littlefield Publishers.

McLaren, P. (2008). Capitalism's bestiary: Rebuilding urban education. In B. Porfilio & C. Malott, (Eds.), *The destructive path of neo-liberalism: An international examination of urban education.* Rotterdam, The Netherlands: Sense Publishers.

McNamara, H., & O'Connor, C. (2006). *Beyond acting white: Reframing the debate on black student achievement.* Lanham, MD: Rowman & Littlefield Publishers.

Mills, C. (1997). *The racial contract.* Ithaca, NY: Cornell University Press.

Mohanty, C. (2003). "Under Western Eyes" revisited: Feminist solidarity through anticapitalist struggles. In C. Mohanty (Ed.), *Feminism without borders: Decolonizing theory, practicing solidarity.* Durham, NC: Duke University Press.

Moll, L. (1988). Some key issues in teaching Latino students. *Language Arts, 65*(5), 465–472.

Montero-Sieburth, M. (2000). The use of cultural resilience in overcoming contradictory encounters in academia: A personal narrative. In E. H. Trueba & L. Bartolome (Eds.), *Immigrant voices: In search of educational equity* (pp. 218–245). Oxford, England: Rowman & Littlefield Publishers.

Moore, M. (2001). *Stupid white men: . . . And other sorry excuses for the state of the nation.* New York, NY: Regan Books.

Myrdal, G. (1944). *An American dilemma: The Negro problem and modern democracy.* New York, NY: Harper & Brothers Publishing.

Nieto, S., & Bode, P. (2011). *Affirming diversity: The sociopolitical context of multicultural education.* Boston, MA: Allyn & Bacon, Inc.

Nkrumah, K. (1965). *Neo-colonialism: The last stage of imperialism.* London, England: Thomas Nelson & Sons, Ltd.

Norton, B. (2000). *Identity and language learning: Gender, ethnicity, and educational change.* London, England: Longman.

Ogbu, J. (1997). Variability in minority response to schooling: Nonimmigrants vs. immigrants. In G. Spindler & L. Spindler (Eds.), *Interpreting ethnographic of education at home and abroad.* Hillsdale, NJ: Lawrence Erlbaum Associates.

Olsen, R. (2003). *Rabbit-Proof Fence* (Motion Picture). Phillip Noyce, Director & Producer.

Orelus, P. W. (2007). *Education under occupation: The heavy price of living in a neocolonized and globalized world.* Rotterdam, The Netherlands: Sense Publishers.

Orelus, P. W. (2009). *The agony of masculinity: Race, gender, and education in the age of "new" racism and patriarchy.* New York, NY: Peter Lang Publishing.

Orelus, P. W. (2010). *Academic achievers: Whose definition? An ethnographic study examining the literacy [under]development of English language learners in the era of high-stakes tests.* Rotterdam, The Netherlands: Sense Publishers.

Orelus, P. W. (2011a). *Rethinking race, class, language, and gender: A dialogue with Noam Chomsky and other leading scholars.* Lanham, MD: Rowman & Littlefield Publishers.

Orelus, P. W. (2011b). *Courageous voices of immigrants and transnationals of color: Counternarratives against discrimination in schools and beyond.* New York, NY: Peter Lang Publishing.

Orelus, P.W. (forthcoming). *The Race Talk: Identity politics, multiracialism, and the hegemony of whiteness.* Charlotte, NC: Information Age Publishing.

Pennycook, A. (2001). *English and the discourses of colonialism.* New York, NY: Routledge.

Phillipson, R. (1992). *Linguistic imperialism.* Oxford, England: Oxford University Press.

Phillipson, R. (2010). *Linguistic imperialism continued.* New York, NY: Routledge.

Plato (2008). *The Republic* (Trans. Robin Waterfield). Oxford, England: Oxford University Press.

Porfilio, B., & Malott, C. (2008). *The destructive path of neo-liberalism: An international examination of urban education.* Rotterdam, The Netherlands: Sense Publishers.

Rickford, R. (2011). *Beyond boundaries: The Manning Marable reader* (Ed.). Boulder, CO: Paradigm Publishers.

Rodney, W. (1972). *How Europe underdeveloped Africa.* Washington, DC: Howard University Press.

Rothenberg, P.S. (2007). *Race, class, and gender in the United States.* New York, NY: Worth Publishers.

Rousseau, J. J. (1966). *Emile ou de L'education.* Paris, France: Garnier-Flammarion.

Rumbaut, R., & Portes, A. (2001). *Ethnicities: Children of immigrants in America.* Berkeley, CA: University of California Press.

Ryan, W. (1976). *Blaming the victim.* New York, NY: Vintage Books.

Said, E. (1978). *Orientalism.* New York, NY: Vintage Books.

Said, E. (1996). *Representations of the intellectuals.* New York, NY: Vintage Books.

Said, E. (2000). *Reflections on exile and other essays.* Cambridge, MA: Harvard University Press.

Schneider, A. (1998). What has happened to faculty diversity in California? *Chronicle of Higher Education, 45*(13), A9–A12.

Semali, L. M. & Kincheloe, J. L. (1999). *What is indigenous knowledge? Voices from the academy.* New York, NY: Falmer Press.

Shierholz, H., & Gould, E. (2011). Poverty and income trends continue to paint a bleak picture for working families. Retrieved from http://www.epi.org/publication/lost-decade-poverty-income-trends-continue

Sleeter, C. E. (2005). *Un-standardizing curriculum: Multicultural teaching in the standardized-based classroom.* New York, NY: Routledge.

Smith, L. T. (1999). *Decolonizing methodologies: Research and indigenous people.* London, England: Zed Books.

Solorzano, D. G. (1998). Critical race theory, racial and gender microaggressions, and the experiences of Chicana and Chicano scholars. *International Journal of Qualitative Studies in Education, 11*, 121–136.

Spivak, G. (1988). Can the subaltern speak? In C. Nelson & L. Grossberg (Eds.), *Marxism and the interpretation of culture.* Chicago, IL: University of Illinois Press.

Spring, J. (2009). *Deculturalization and the struggle for equality: A brief history of the education of dominated cultures in the United States* (6th ed.). New York: McGraw-Hill Humanities/Social Sciences/Languages.

Stilson, J. (Director). (2009). *Good hair* [Motion picture]. United States: Lionsgate.

Stovall, D. (2006). Forging community in race and class: Critical race and the quest for social justice in education. *Race, ethnicity, and education, 9*(3), 243–259.

Subreenduth, S. (2008). Deconstructing the politics of a differently colored transnational identity. *Race, Ethnicity and Education, 11*(1), 41–55.
Tatum, B. D. (2003). *"Why are all the black kids sitting together in the cafeteria?": A psychologist explains the development of racial identity.* New York, NY: Basic Books.
Tatum, B. D. (2007). *Can we talk about race? And other conversations in an era of school resegregation.* Boston, MA: Beacon Press.
Taylor, G. (2004). *Buying whiteness: Race, culture and identity from Columbus to hip-hop.* New York, NY: Palgrave Macmillan.
Teresi, D. (2002). *Lost discoveries: The ancient roots of modern science—from the Babylonians to the Maya.* New York, NY: Simon & Schuster Paperbacks.
Tyson, K. (2011). *Integration interrupted: Tracking, black students, and acting white after Brown.* Oxford, England: Oxford University Press.
Valdés, G. (2001). *Learning and not learning English: Latino students in American schools.* New York, NY: Teachers College Press.
Valdés, G., Capitelli, S., & Alvarez, L. (2010). *Latino children learning English: Steps in the journey.* New York, NY: Teachers College Press.
Vygotsky, L. (1978). *Mind in society.* Cambridge, MA: Harvard University Press.
wa Thiong'o, N. (1986). *Decolonizing the mind: The politics of language in African literature.* Portsmouth, NH: Heinemann Educational Books, Inc.
Wane, N. N. (2006). Is decolonization possible? In G. S. Dei & A. Kempf (Eds.), *Anticolonialism and education: The politics of resistance* (pp. 87–106). Rotterdam, The Netherlands: Sense Publishers.
West, C. (1993). *Race matters.* Cambridge, MA: Beacon Press.
West, C. (2004). *Democracy matters: Winning the fight against imperialism.* New York, NY: Penguin Press.
Williams, E. (1993). *History of the people of Trinidad and Tobago.* Brooklyn, NY: A&B Publishers.
Wise, T. (2011). *White like me: Reflections on race from a privileged son.* Berkeley, CA: Soft Skull Press.
Yosso, T. J. (2006). *Critical race counterstories along the Chicana/Chicano educational pipeline.* New York, NY: Routledge.
Young, R. (2006). *Postcolonialism: An historical introduction.* Malden, MA: Blackwell Publishing.
Zirin, D. (2009). *People's history of sports in the United States: 250 years of politics, protest, people, and play.* New York, NY: The New Press.

Index

A

Abdi, Ali Ix, 9, 85
Acuña, Rodolfo 55, 85
Adelson, Leanne v, vii
Ahmed, Sara 54, 85
Aldama, Arturo 55, 85
Alexander, Bryant 5, 85
Alexander, Michelle 14, 15, 32, 85
Anzaldúa, Gloria 33, 37, 38, 54, 55, 85, 86
Appiah, Kwame A. 54, 86
Aronowitz, Stanley 32, 86
Asante, Molefi 9, 15, 22, 83, 86
Auerbach, Elsa R. 48, 86
Austin, Algernon 16, 17, 86

B

Baird, Forrest 30, 86
Bakhtin, Mikhail 44, 86
Bell, Derrick 17, 55, 86

Bell, Lee A. 65, 86
Biko, Steve x, xiii, 13, 22, 24, 86
Bonilla-Silva, Eduardo xvi, xx, 2, 15, 16, 23, 86
Bourdieu, Pierre xx, 21, 38, 86
Byrd, Ayana 3, 86

C

Cabral, Amílcar 9, 24, 86
Cain, Carole 54, 89
Carr, Paul R. vii, xvii, xx, 2, 13, 30, 37, 86, 87
Castells, Manuel 54, 87
Césaire, Aimé xi, 24, 87
Chomsky, Noam xii, 30, 32, 34, 35, 36, 37, 68, 83, 87, 88, 91, 92
Churchill, Ward 33, 87
Collins, Patricia H. 68, 83, 91
Coloma, Roland S. 55, 87
Cook, Michael xi, 87
Crawford, James 32, 33, 87

Crenshaw, Kimberle xiv, 56, 87, 91
Cummins, Jim 32, 33, 87

D

Darder, Antonia xiii, 29, 38, 68, 83, 87, 89
Davis, Angela 3, 14, 68
Davis, Troy xix, xx
De Tocqueville, Alexis 33, 87
Dei, George Sefa, xvi, xx, 1, 2, 9, 13, 42, 75, 87, 89, 90, 94
Delgado, Richard 55, 56, 63, 88, 91
Denzin, Norman K. 30, 85, 88, 89
Dewey, John 30, 31, 44, 48, 68, 82, 83, 88
Dillard, Cynthia 2, 3, 4, 5, 88
Diop, Cheikh Anta 24, 88
Douglass, Frederick 24, 25, 88
Du Bois, W. E. B. 13, 23, 24, 64, 88

E

Ellis, Carolyn 5, 88

F

Fairlie, Robert 16, 88
Fanon, Frantz x, xi, 9, 11, 23, 24, 32, 42, 53, 57, 58, 71, 83, 88
Fedigan, Jay 88
Firmin, Antenor 14, 15, 24, 25, 88
Foucault, Michel 38, 55, 88
Freire, Paulo 31, 43, 45, 48, 51, 55, 68, 83, 89

G

Gillborn, David 55, 86, 89, 90
Giroux, Henry 30, 31, 32, 68, 89
Gobineau, Arthur 24, 89
Gramsci, Antonio 38, 39, 42, 89
Grande, Sandy 33, 68, 89
Grant, Carl 49, 87, 89
Greene, Maxine 31, 89

H

Hall, Stuart 19, 83, 89
Hamzeh, Manal 54, 89
Harris, Cheryl 19, 89
Herrnstein, Richard 24, 89
Hirsch, E. D. 34, 89
Holland, Dorothy 54, 89
Holman Jones, Stacy xvi, 5, 89
hooks, bell 3, 54, 55, 68, 71, 83, 89, 90
Husband, Terry 5, 90
Hutardo, Aida 19, 90

J

Jensen, Arthur R. 24, 90
Jensen, Robert 1, 2, 90

K

Kaufmann, Walter 30, 86
Kempf, Arlo 42, 75, 88, 90, 94
Kendall, Frances E. 2, 90
Kincheloe, Joe 68, 76, 89, 93
Klein, Naomi 32, 90
Kneller, George F. 44, 45, 90
Kozol, Jonathan xv, 19, 20, 21, 68, 90

L

Lachicotte Jr., William 54, 89
Ladson-Billings, Gloria 55, 86, 90
Lavia, Jennifer 5, 90
Leistyna, Pepi 32, 62, 90
Leonardo, Zeus 2, 16, 55, 64, 90, 91
Lipman, Pauline 31, 91
Loewen, James 22, 91
Loomba, Ania 41, 42, 91
Lopez, Alfred 1, 91
Lumumba, Patrice 22
Lund, Darren E. vii, xx, 2, 13, 86, 87

M

Macedo, Donaldo 18, 20, 29, 30, 32, 33, 53, 61, 62, 63, 68, 90, 91
Martin, Trayvon xx, 17
Marx, Karl 39, 91
Matsuda, Mari 56, 91
McIntosh, Peggy 2, 19, 91
McLaren, Peter 32, 44, 68, 83, 89, 91
McNamara, Erin 2, 91
Mills, Charles xiii, 15, 91
Mohanty, Chandra 55, 92
Moll, Luis 39, 92
Montero-Sieburth, Martha 54, 92
Moore, Michael 19, 92
Murray, Charles 24, 89
Myrdal, Gunnar 33, 92

N

Nieto, Sonia 49, 62, 83, 92
Nkrumah, Kwame 42, 92
Norton, Bonny 54, 87, 92

O

Obama, Barack 14, 16, 26, 67
Ogbu, John 9, 92
Olsen, Christine 33, 92
Orelus, Frida vii
Orelus, Lyonel vii
Orelus, Pierre vi, ix, x, xi, xii, xiv, xv, 4, 23, 25, 31, 34, 35, 36, 39, 42, 62, 63, 64, 65, 71, 72, 73, 78, 79, 80, 81, 82, 83, 88, 91, 92

P

Pacheco, Romina vii
p'Biket Okot x
Pennycook, Alastair 63, 92
Phillipson, Robert xxi, 61, 63, 92

Plato 30, 31, 45, 86, 93
Porfilio, Bradley 32, 87, 91, 93

R

Rickford, Russell 13, 45, 93
Rodney, Walter 9, 33, 93
Rothenberg, Paula xiv, 93
Rousseau, Jean-Jacques 44, 93
Rumbaut, Rubén 56, 93
Ryan, William 21, 93

S

Said, Edward 9, 55, 68, 83, 93
Schneider, Alison 63, 93
Semali, Ladislaus 76, 93
Shierholz, Heidi 16, 17, 93
Sleeter, Christine 31, 49, 89, 93
Smith, Linda Tuhiwai 55, 93
Solorzano, Daniel xv, 93
Spivak, Gayatri C. 37, 55, 93
Spring, Joel 33, 93
Stilson, Jeff 3, 93
Stefancic, Jean 55, 88
Stovall, David 55, 93
Subreenduth, Sharon 64, 94
Sundstrom, William, 16, 88

T

Tatum, Beverly 17, 18, 19, 94
Taylor, Gary ix, 86, 94
Teresi, Dick 22, 94
Tharps, Lori 3, 86
Torres, Myriam 68
Tyson, Karolyn 2, 94

V

Valdés, Guadalupe 32, 56, 94
Vygotsky, Lev 31, 48, 94

W

wa Thiong'o, Ngugi 41, 42, 53, 62, 63, 71, 94
Wane, Njoki N. 75, 76, 94
West, Cornel xvii, 33, 68, 85, 94
Williams, Eric 34, 94
Winfrey, Oprah 3
Wise, Tim 1, 2, 94

Y

Yosso, Tara 15, 94
Young, Robert 42, 54, 94

Z

Zirin, Dave 19, 94